MORNE-PAYSAN

Peasant Village in Martinique

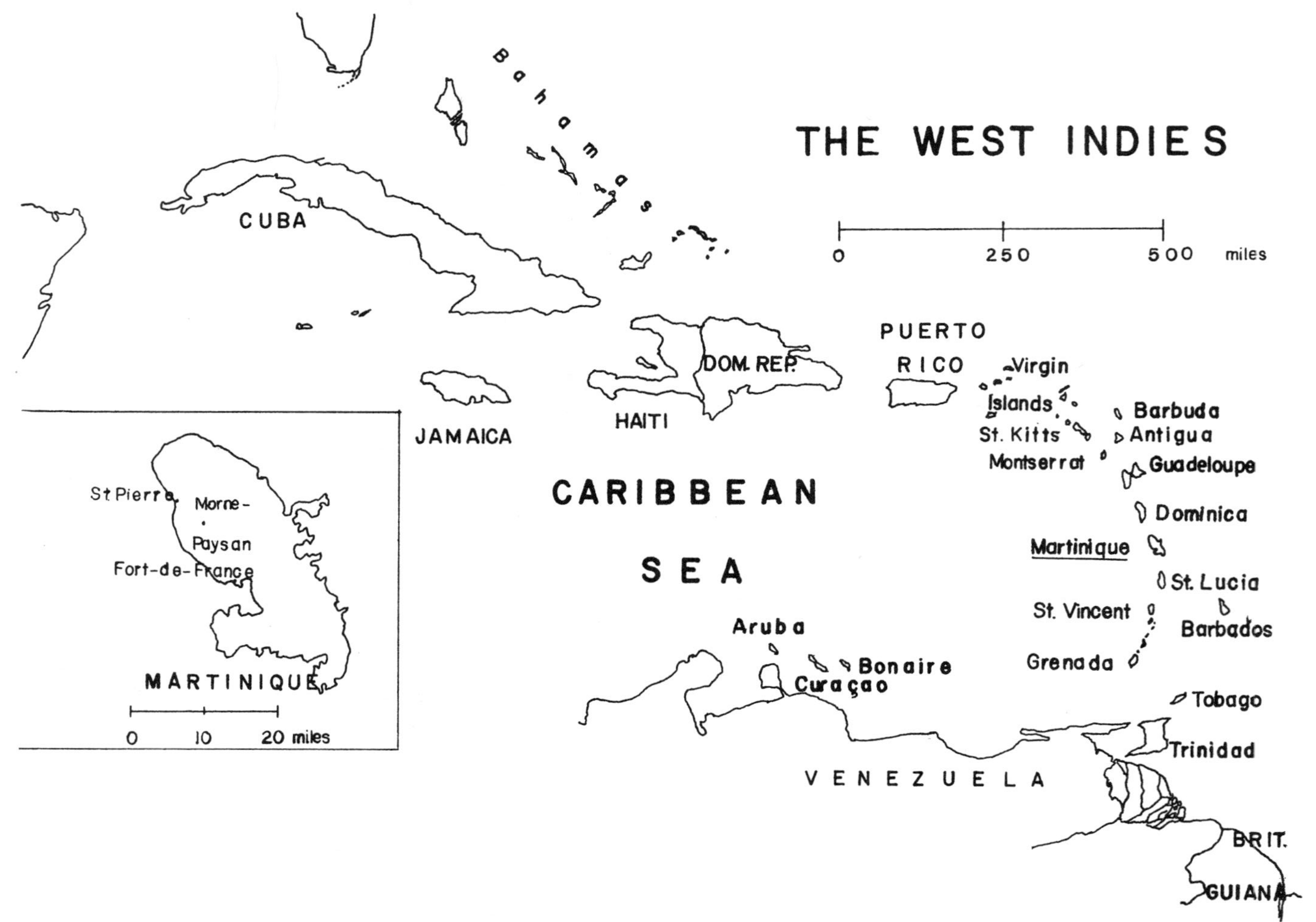
THE WEST INDIES
0
250
500
miles
Bahamas
CUBA
JAMAICA
HAITI
DOM. REP.
PUERTO
RICO
Virgin
Islands
St. Kitts
Montserrat
Barbuda
Antigua
Guadeloupe
Dominica
Martinique
St. Lucia
St. Vincent
Barbados
Grenada
Tobago
Trinidad
CARIBBEAN
SEA
Aruba
Curaçao
Bonaire
VENEZUELA
BRIT.
GUIANA
St Pierre
Morne-
Paysan
Fort-de-France
MARTINIQUE
0
10
20 miles

MORNE-PAYSAN

Peasant Village in Martinique

By

MICHAEL M. HOROWITZ

Prospect Heights, Illinois

For information about this book, write or call:
Waveland Press, Inc.
P.O. Box 400
Prospect Heights, Illinois 60070
(708) 634-0081

1992 reissued with changes by Waveland Press, Inc.

ISBN 0-88133-683-1

Printed in the United States of America

7 6 5 4 3 2 1

To my mother,
and the memory of my father.

Foreword

About the Author

Michael Horowitz is Professor of Anthropology at the State University of New York at Binghamton and Director of the Institute for Development Anthropology. In addition to fieldwork in Martinique and elsewhere in the Caribbean, he has carried out anthropological research among farmers, fishers, and herders in Niger, Mali, Senegal, Sudan, Rwanda, Zimbabwe, and Tunisia. He has been a senior social science adviser to the World Bank, the United Nations Development Programme, the UN Development Fund for Women, the UN Conference on Environment and Development, the UN Environment Programme, the UN Food and Agriculture Organization, the US Congress Office of Technology Assessment, the National Academy of Sciences, the Agency for International Development, and the Overseas Development Council. He has written and edited many books and articles on the relationship between anthropology and socioeconomic development in the Third World.

About the Book

This case study requires little introduction. Written clearly and succinctly it presents a well-rounded picture of life in one inland agricultural village in Martinique, an island of the West Indies. High points of Dr. Horowitz's treatment include a detailed discussion of household composition, a matter of special interest in Caribbean ethnology; an analysis of agriculture and markets; a discussion of factions and conflicts within the village as related to religion, economics, and politics; and a description of the round of life from birth to death. Though notable for the objective documentation of generalizations, the case study does not lose sight of the human characteristics of the people.

Particularly valuable is the historical and comparative perspective provided in this study. The present situation of Morne-Paysan is seen as a derivative of colonization, emancipation, and industrialization. The village is a product of history and today represents processes, such as the proletarianization of the peasantry, that are occurring throughout the Caribbean, and indeed wherever such populations exist throughout the world. The comparative perspective is enhanced by an explicit comparison with other Caribbean villages exhibiting similarities and differences in socioeconomic structure, political status, and ethnic composition. One can see Morne-Paysan as a variant upon a basic Caribbean theme.

GEORGE AND LOUISE SPINDLER

Preface

My fieldwork in the French West Indies in 1956, 1957–1958, 1962, and 1964 was supported by fellowships and grants from the Social Science Research Council, the Man in the Tropics program of the Research Institute for the Study of Man, the Department of Anthropology at Columbia University, and the Research Foundation of State University of New York. I was able to revisit Martinique very briefly in May 1966. The "ethnographic present" for the descriptive material of Morne-Paysan (a fictive name of a real village) is 1956–1958.

I first learned about the West Indies from George Eaton Simpson, of Oberlin College, who has devoted almost thirty years to anthropological inquiry in Haiti, Jamaica, and Trinidad. My teachers, Conrad M. Arensberg, Elliott P. Skinner, and Charles Wagley, of Columbia University, guided my studies in graduate school, and encouraged and supported the research in the field.

Many people in Martinique and in the United States took a deep and serious interest in this work. I may single out for grateful acknowledgment only a few. Heartfelt thanks are due Dr. Jean Benoist, Alexandre and Anca Bertrand, Marie-Annick Blanc, Guy Chalono, Feriez Elisabeth, Gabriel Vincent and Lisette Jacques, Morton and Sheila Klass, Alain Plénel, Jacques Senet, and Roland Suvélor. They have shared with me not only their profound insight, but also their homes, tables, and friendship.

My colleagues, Melvin M. Leiman, Harpur College, and Otto Blehr, University of Bergen, Norway, critically read and commented on Chapters 4 and 8 respectively. Sidney W. Mintz, Yale University, read Chapters 2 through 8, and gave me the benefit of his intimate understanding of the Caribbean. My debt to him is very great. Those deficiencies which remain in this book are entirely my own responsibility.

My wife, Sylvia Huntley Horowitz, participated at every stage of the fieldwork, and has applied her editorial skills to my prose; whatever grace may be on these pages reflects her educated sense of diction. In the field, with no formal preparation, she established those warm and sincere relationships with the people without which one may have informants but not friends.

MICHAEL M. HOROWITZ

Bergen, Norway
February 1967

Foreword 1992

by William Miles, *Northeastern University*

Why reissue *Morne-Paysan* today, twenty-five years after its original publication? Since 1967, when Professor Michael Horowitz' classic text on a peasant village in Martinique was originally published, the village which Horowitz calls "Morne-Paysan" has undergone considerable transformation. The theoretical framework out of which *Morne-Paysan* originally emerged has also undergone a sea of change. In light of these changes—the one social, the other academic—original analysis of Morne-Paysan has spawned some fairly intense debate.[1] Thus, republishing *Morne-Paysan* in the 1990s borders on the anthropologically provocative. Only when alerted to this larger context can the reader fully appreciate the import and contribution of *Morne-Paysan* to ongoing scholarship on the French West Indies and the evolution of social science paradigms.

A visitor to Morne-Vert today will not easily recognize the village described in the third, fourth, and fifth chapters of *Morne-Paysan*.[2] Homes are no longer the wattle-and-daub, thatched roof, and earthen floor *gaulettes* of the 1950s. For sure, they are now electrified—T.V. antennas attest to that. Men today are more likely to wear tee-shirts and jeans than "large straw hats" and peasant-style trousers. Adults no longer go shoeless and preschool children are properly clad. The two roads leading up to Morne-Vert from the coast have ceased being so perilous and, in contrast to the scarcity of motorized transport that Horowitz reports, today greater frustration arises from traffic jams in the village center (particularly when school lets out). In short, "development"—or some version of it—has transformed the outward appearance of Morne-Vert.

More important than these superficial changes, the agricultural system that Horowitz so perceptibly describes—the very foundation of Morne-Vert's peasant economy—has undergone a serious shock. Greater integration into the French (and soon European) economy has dealt a heavy blow to the indigenous, material foundation of Martiniquan society. As throughout the rest of the island, real estate has become more important than cropland. Residential pressures have marginalized and in many instances replaced farmland. Although fieldwork is still more often performed by farmers than by researchers, village dependence on agricultural marketing has waned considerably.

The second *problématique* of *Morne-Paysan*'s rebirth is the theoretical applicability of the original monograph. Exemplar of the "community studies" model of its era, artfully crafting an ethnographic picture of a clearly delimited micro-society, this classic approach to anthropological inquiry has been largely subsumed by the "political economy" perspective, a perspective that Horowitz himself has also espoused.[3] Individual case studies are useful to political economy but only insofar as they help illustrate wider economic processes, systems, and international structures of power. Whether Morne-Vert (and Martinique) are more accurately recast within a "plantation" or "bureaucratic economy" framework remains moot: that there is a broader context (be it insular, national, or international) within which it must be framed is undeniable. This is the perspective that even a recent *urban* analysis of Martiniquan society has adopted.[4]

Within the English language, the political evolution of the French West Indies as a whole has provided the most extensive literature for students of Martinique. Whether it be in terms of political integration,[5] national independence,[6] or electoral participation,[7] post-Horowitzian presentations of Martinique have been invariably political in orientation. So the question remains: What does this description of life in a single, peasant village of Martinique contribute today?

An immense amount.

For one thing, all of the above-mentioned studies have built, implicitly or directly, on *Morne-Paysan*. Michael Horowitz is must reading for anyone interested in this part of the world. He is also must reading for those wishing to trace the intellectual evolution within anthropology from community studies to political economy to—whatever paradigm comes next. If it is a structure-agent paradigm—one that recognizes the role of individual actors as coequal with impersonal forces and processes—the personalistic description of Martiniquan society that *Morne-Paysan* exemplifies will be even more apropos. Even if community studies have been transcended as a methodological approach, the point that individuals are *also* members of local communities, and that the systemic changes that affect local communities also affect individuals, is a worthwhile reminder.

For this is the second important contribution of Horowitz' book. It is a reminder that social studies (taken in its widest meaning) is about people. That the names used in *Morne-Paysan* are fictionalized is inconsequential. We know that they are identifiable persons. Even if two and a half decades later the children have become adults, the adults have become old, and the old have passed on, Horowitz' "ethnographic present" remains a timeless, sympathetic portrayal of a Caribbean lifestyle that can never disappear. Merge into the present, yes. Transform and adapt to wider societal processes (such as departmentalization within the French Republic and integration into the European Community), yes. But the social foundation of Morne-Vert, and for that matter most West Indian society *in extensu* (see his Chapter 9), remains connected to that post-slavery, peasant-based, Creole culture to which Horowitz elegantly introduces us.

Thirdly, the careful reader of *Morne-Paysan* will find not only a perspicacious foreshadowing of societal transformation still then awaiting Morne-Vert, but an anticipation of the political-economic analysis that was developed in the decade following its publication. In reading about Morne-Paysan the reader should note what Horowitz says not only about the village itself but about economic processes and trends beyond Morne-Paysan. *Morne-Paysan* is much more than a description of one village on one island in the Caribbean. It is a model of the anthropological method, a sterling representation of academic rigor combined with understated wit and human empathy.

Endnotes

[1] William F. S. Miles, "Martinique and Morne-Vert: French 'Departmentalization' or Caribbean 'Plantation Economy'? A Third Look at the Baber-Horowitz Debate," *Anthropology* 10 (1986):19-32; "Reply to Baber," following Willie L. Baber, "Political Economy and the Plantation System: A Note on the Baber-Horowitz Debate," *Anthropology* 10 (1986):33-42.

[2] Morne-Paysan was revealed to be a pseudonym of Morne-Vert in Willie L. Baber, "Social Change and the Peasant Community: Horowitz' Morne-Paysan Reinterpreted," *Ethnology* 21 (1982):227-240. See also Baber's "Political Process in Morne-Vert: A Note on the Economizing Strategy," *Anthropology* 8 (1984):1-11 and "Land Tenure and Class in Morne-Vert," *Anthropology* 8 (1985):41-54.

[3] See, for instance, "Donors and Deserts: The Political Ecology of Destructive Development in the Sahel," in *African Food Systems in Crisis. Part 2. Contending with Change*, R. Huss-Ashmore and S. H. Katz, eds. (New York and London: Gordon and Breach) 1990; "The Political Economy of Desertification in White Nile Province, Sudan," with Muneera Salem-Murdock, in *Lands at Risk in the Third World*, Peter D. Little and Michael M. Horowitz, eds. (Boulder, CO: Westview Press) 1987.

[4] Michel S. Laguerre, *Urban Poverty in the Caribbean: French Martinique as a Social Laboratory* (New York: St. Martin's Press) 1990.

[5] Arvin Murch, *Black Frenchmen: The Political Integration of the French Antilles* (Cambridge, MA: Schenkman Publishing Co.) 1971; "Political Integration as an Alternative to Independence in the French Antilles," *American Sociological Review* 33 (1968):544-62.

[6] Richard D. E. Burton, *Assimilation or Independence? Prospects for Martinique* (Montreal: McGill University, Centre for Developing-Area Studies, Occasional Monograph Series, No. 13) 1978.

[7] William F. S. Miles, *Elections and Ethnicity in French Martinique: A Paradox in Paradise* (New York: Praeger Publishers) 1986; "Mitterrand in the Caribbean: Socialism (?) Comes to Martinique," *Journal of Interamerican Studies and World Affairs* 27 (1985):63-79; "Electoral Flip-Flop in the French Caribbean," *French Politics and Society* 8 (1990):39-52.

Market specialist, *revendeuse,* in Fort-de-France.

Contents

Foreword vii
Preface viii
Foreword 1992 *by William Miles* ix

1. The Anthropology of the West Indies 1

2. An Historical View 9
Precolonists, 9
French Colonization, 10

3. The Village 17

4. The Fields 24
Agricultural Crops and Rhythms, 24
Holdings and Tenure, 29
Productive Groups, 32
Markets, 33

5. The Household 39
The Sample, 40
Varieties of Domestic Units, 43
A Case Study of Household Variation, 45

6. The Round of Life: Marriage and Other Matings 51

7. The Round of Life: Birth to Death 59
Birth and Childhood, 59
Adolescence and Adulthood, 65
Health, 67
Death, 74

8. Consensus and Conflict 79

Religion, 81
Economics, 86
Politics, 88
Courts, 91

9. Some Other Caribbean Villages 95

Guianese Villages, 95
August Town, 95
Canalville, 97
The Puerto Rican Municipio, 98
Tabara, 98
Cañamelar, 101
Peasant and Plantation in Jamaica, 103
Summary, 104

10. The Future of the Martiniquan Peasantry 106

Glossary 109

References 111

Recommended Reading 113

1

The Anthropology of the West Indies

At first glance it is curious that any anthropological work has been done in the West Indies at all, for there are almost no indigenous people, the *sine qua non* of traditional ethnological inquiry. And yet the area has seized the imagination of some of the most influential American anthropologists of the last thirty years. There are no indigenes at all in most of the islands, and just a pitiful remnant of the Caribs in Dominica. An early consequence of European colonization during the sixteenth and seventeenth centuries was the almost total destruction of the Indians. The destroyers were Western Europeans: Spaniards, Englishmen, Scotsmen, Dutchmen, Normands, Bretons. Then came the Africans by the millions, captured, transported, sold, and enslaved on New World estates during three hundred years. The slave-based plantation effectively blocked further substantial European migration, for the potential migrant could rarely sustain the capital expenses to acquire the necessary land, labor, and machinery. Slavery was everywhere abolished during the nineteenth century, and in a few places new immigrants, indentured workers from India, Africa, China, and other countries, came to labor on the estates. Thus the Caribbean islands were colonial possessions, properties of European states, but with no colonized peoples: the people were all colonists!

The West Indies are unusual economically as well. Most of them at one time or another took the form of vast agrarian factories, or plantations, producing a very special series of crops designed for overseas consumption: sugar, cacao, tobacco, spices, rum, and coffee, "effective fare for the factory workers of Britain and France, quelling their hunger pangs and numbing their outrage" (Mintz 1964*a:* xvii). The recurrent pattern of land exploitation was the plantation, worked by Negro slaves who had no control over the production and distribution of the crops. After emancipation the now freedmen were salaried, forming the first great agrarian proletariat, with no enhanced access to economic decision-making. Their lot resembled more that of the wage laborers in the emerging factories of Europe than that of the European peasants, or even the peasants of North Africa, South Asia, and the Far East.

These then are the central facts or common experiences of the West Indies. First, they are insular and most of them are small. Cuba, some 90 miles off the Florida coast, is the largest and most populous, with an area of about 44,000 square miles and a population of about seven million. The next largest is Hispaniola, with 28,000 square miles distributed between Haiti and the Dominican Republic. Jamaica has only a tenth the area of Cuba, with about 4400 square miles, and Puerto Rico, the easternmost of the large islands or Greater Antilles, has a surface of some 3400 square miles. The islands of the Lesser Antilles run south from Puerto Rico, forming the eastern border of the Caribbean Sea. They range in size from Trinidad which, with its dependency Tobago, has slightly less than 2000 square miles, down to the tiny islets of the Grenadines of a few square miles each.

The Lesser Antilles, in particular, have two major characteristics of "island ecosystems" (Fosberg 1963:5): limited size and relative isolation. Martinique, for example, measures about 40 miles by 20 miles at its greatest extensions, and is separated from its neighbors Dominica to the north and St. Lucia to the south by some 20 miles of rough seas. By virtue of intensive human occupation for more than 400 years, these islands do not have the features of closed, relatively stable biotic communities. Instead the environments are continuously and rapidly changing. Not only has there been a succession of diverse nonaboriginal human populations—in Martinique, Caribs replaced Arawaks shortly before the Europeans arrived, then French, Africans, East Indians, other Europeans, and Syrians (a generic term for immigrants from the French-speaking areas of North Africa and Southwest Asia); the immigrants brought with them new crops, new animals, and new planting techniques. Sugar, bananas, pineapples, breadfruit, mangoes, and many other typically West Indian cultigens were introduced from the Old World, along with cows, pigs, chickens, sheep, goats, and horses.

The emphasis on monocrop production in a number of the islands has rendered them particularly vulnerable to economic and natural disasters. Hurricanes, endemic in the region, are especially damaging to fragile banana trees. The economic vulnerability of monocrop production is caused by an inability of the colonies to control external events. The major crisis faced, and faced periodically, was the opening up of competitive lands or new sources of the crop. Martinique and Guadeloupe experienced their great crisis in the nineteenth century, with the development of the beet sugar industry in France. Over the next hundred years, increasing amounts of land were shifted from cane to bananas, but here the islands have had to face not only competition from each other, but also from African areas dominated by French commercial interests, such as the Ivory Coast. Production and export quotas are assigned in relationship to external conditions, rather than to domestic capabilities.

The second common experience of the Antilles is their colonial history. With the single exception of Haiti, which achieved its independence by revolution in 1803, all the islands remained colonies until the twentieth century. Many of them changed hands frequently. Spain, the original colonizer, lost much of her empire to England and France in the seventeenth and eighteenth centuries, and the remainder to the United States at the end of the nineteenth century. Of these, Cuba and the Dominican Republic were nominally independent, but in fact were under United States domination for much of the 20th century. Even Scandinavia had colonies. Sweden administered St. Bartolemy for almost a hundred years, before returning it to France in 1877. Denmark sold its little colonies, the Virgin Islands, to the United States in 1917. One consequence of this multiplicity of colonial powers is a tremendously complex legal heritage.

The population, area, and current political affiliations of the more prominent islands are listed in the following table:

TABLE 1

THE WEST INDIES IN 1958

Island	Area (square miles)	Population*	Political Affiliation**
Cuba	44,200	6,587,000	Republic
Jamaica	4,400	1,542,000	United Kingdom
Haiti	10,200	3,979,000	Republic
Dominican Republic	18,700	2,800,000	Republic
Puerto Rico	3,400	2,299,000	United States
American Virgin Islands			United States
St. Thomas	32	15,000	
St. Croix	82	14,000	
St. John	19	1,000	
St. Maarten, Saba, St. Eustatius	28	5,000	Netherlands
Leeward Islands			United Kingdom
British Virgin Islands	67	8,000	
St. Kitts-Nevis-Anguilla	158	58,000	
Antigua, Barbuda, Redonda	171	57,000	
Montserrat	32	14,000	
Guadeloupe and Dependencies	690	257,000	France
Martinique	385	264,000	France
Windward Islands			United Kingdom
Dominica	305	65,000	
St. Lucia	223	92,000	
St. Vincent	150	80,000	
Grenada and Grenadines	160	91,000	
Barbados	166	235,000	United Kingdom
Trinidad and Tobago	1,980	789,000	United Kingdom
Aruba, Bonaire, Curaçao	390	182,000	Netherlands

* 1958 population estimates from *United Nations Statistical Yearbook 1964*.

** The principal political changes since 1958 have been the independence of Barbados, Jamaica and Trinidad, following the unsuccessful attempt at Federation of the former British West Indies; and the overthrow of governments in Cuba and the Dominican Republic.

Economically this colonialism made the islands classic examples of mercantilism. They produce raw materials—food crops, tobacco, and cotton—for export, and import all processed and manufactured goods from the mother country and by means of transport controlled by the mother country. Sea-island cotton from the British Leewards is spun into thread, woven into cloth, and cut and sewn into garments in Europe; a shirt of sea-island cotton costs more in Antigua than in England. The sugar exported from most of the islands is brown, with a heavy molasses content. It is refined in Europe and the United States and white sugar is an expensive luxury in the Caribbean. West Indian tobacco is processed in European cigarette factories; and so on.

Colonialism has had other effects as well. Politically it has meant that the islands are governed from abroad and administered locally by persons sent from abroad. (Colonial service has been a means for rapid and well-paid advancement through the ranks of the British, French, and Dutch governments.) Although there was greater use of local personnel in the British administration, generally the upper levels were effectively closed to all but metropolitans and a handful of creole whites. Educationally, colonialism has meant the imposition of metropolitan curricula, texts, and examinations in local schools. Children learn the history and geography of the metropole, and are ignorant of their own. "One hundred years before Christ, the Germans came to our land . . ." begins a textbook used in the Dutch Windwards in 1958 (Keur and Keur 1960:193). British West Indian pupils have to learn arithmetic problems in terms of pounds, shillings, and pence, even though the local units of currency are dollars and cents. Martiniquan students are taught that in winter the snow accumulates on the fallen leaves, while they are expected to know nothing of the geography of Guadeloupe. West Indian nationalism as it emerged following the Second World War differed from the early nationalisms of Ireland, India, and the Arab lands, for example, and the contemporary nationalisms of Africa and other parts of Asia, in its general avoidance of nativism and the evocation of its own past. The metropolitan colonial country remains the model of intellectual excellence in the Caribbean.

The third common experience of the West Indies is their tendency to be stratified into two great sections: a dominant planter class, owning or managing the estate lands, and controlling the import-export trade and a subordinate agricultural proletariat. With the prominent exceptions of Cuba, Puerto Rico and the Dominican Republic, these two sections are usually distinguished as well by color: the darker-skinned descendants of slaves and indentured laborers still form the mass of the proletariat, and the lighter-skinned descendants of the slaveowners from the bulk of the controlling class. (The Spanish-speaking colonies developed differently in part because Spain was much more involved in its mainland Central and South American operations, and paid less attention to its Caribbean possessions.) In a number of islands, a buffer group of men of color, typically with white fathers and black mothers, emerged in positions intermediary between those of the top and bottom. Hence, the system of stratification resembles a color-class pyramid, dark at the base, and lightening toward the apex. With the advent of local autonomy and independence in some of the islands, there was a separation between political and economic power. Persons of color acceded to those political positions which were open to the ballot, but the whites continued to dominate the economic sector.

While these common facts unite the islands, and permit us to consider them as a culture area, there are important differences among them which should not be obscured. These differences obtain in the peculiar geographic, economic, ethnic, racial, and colonial experiences which they have had. Writing only of the British West Indies, Lowenthal outlines their various productive activities (1958:339):

> Agriculture remains the mainstay of the area, but Jamaica also relies heavily on bauxite and Trinidad on oil. Sugar monopolizes only Barbados, St. Kitts, and, to a smaller extent, Antigua; bananas, cacao, coconuts, and citrus fruits occupy more and more land and people in Jamaica, Trinidad, and the Windwards; and several islands depend on unusual specialties—Grenada on nutmegs, St. Vincent on arrowroot, Montserrat on sea-island cotton.

Tobacco is an important crop in Cuba, the Dominican Republic, and Puerto Rico, and coffee is the leading export of Haiti. The Dutch Windwards are exporters of manpower rather than produce, sending men to the oil fields of Aruba and Curaçao and to the merchant marine. St. Thomas is devoted almost exclusively to tourism, and some of the small islands in the Leewards are increasingly geared to visitors.

Colonial political groupings do not neatly define cultural ones. For example, Guadeloupe, Dominica, Martinique and St. Lucia form a linguistic unit whose populations speak mutually intelligible creoles, similar to the language of Haiti, which are not understood by metropolitan English and French. The common tongues of St. Martin, an island administered severally by France and Holland, are English and Papiamento, the patois of Curaçao. Schoolteachers sent to these islands from the mother countries are unable to communicate with many of their pupils.

What kinds of researches have anthropologists made in the West Indies? M. G. Smith, himself one of the most creative Caribbean schoiars, brilliantly reviews and criticizes the contributions of other social scientists in "A Framework for Caribbean Studies" (1955), an essential paper for anyone planning research in the area. I shall merely outline, therefore, the major trends, mention some of the more prominent workers, and refer the reader to Smith's paper for detailed analysis.

While studies of folklore predate his work, Melville J. Herskovits was the first to essay anthropologically significant field research in the Caribbean. Herskovits was concerned with broad problems of cultural persistence and change. His thesis that New World Negroes were not without a meaningful past, but participated in a culture whose roots lay in the African continent from which they were stolen, was contrary to much of the opinion of his day. He saw in the values and behaviours of his Dutch Guianian, Haitian, and Trinidadian informants connections which antedated slavery. Not all these connections were simple survivals, in which the African and West Indian instances of the event were to all purposes identical; in fact, Herskovits felt that few such survivals would be found. More often the event was "syncretized" in a new setting, containing elements of both the African and European traditions, as in the Vodun religion of Haiti or the Shango of Trinidad, where West African and Christian pantheons merge at certain points, and the adepts assert clear equations between them. Even more remote from the original form are "reinterpretations," in which the African source is discovered beneath the surface. Herskovits felt that the sequence of matings or serial monogamy frequently reported in descriptions of New World Negro families was a reinterpretation of West Africa polygyny:

> As for the father, he continued to play for the nuclear group the institutionally re-

> mote, humanly somewhat secondary role that in Africa was his as the parent shared with the children of other mothers than one's own, a role that was transmuted into the more or less transitory position he holds in so many of the poorer families of New World Negro societies (Herskovits 1947:16). This also explains the importance of the household in the rearing and training of children. In essence, this is based on the retention in Toco [Trinidad] of the nucleus of African kinship structures which . . . consists of a mother and her children living in a hut within her husband's compound, also inhabited by her co-wives and their children. That this nuclear unit has evolved into such a household as the one headed by the elderly woman . . . where her grown daughters are still more or less under her direction and some of their children entirely given over to her care, merely represents in one respect the logical development of this African institution under the influence of slavery and of the particular socio-economic position of the Negroes after slavery was abolished (Herskovits 1947:295–296).

To some other scholars, the conditions of slavery were so pervasive that continuity with the African past was irrevocably severed. To them, it is slavery itself which explains the female-centered lower-class Negro household:

> When sexual taboos and restraints imposed by their original culture were lost, the behavior of the slaves in this regard was subject at first only to the control of the masters and the wishes of those selected for mates. Hence, on the large plantations, where the slaves were treated almost entirely as instruments of production and brute force was relied upon as the chief means of control, sexual relations were likely to be dissociated on the whole from human sentiments and feelings. Then too, the constant buying and selling of slaves prevented the development of strong emotional ties between the mates. But, where slavery became a settled way of life, the slaves were likely to show preferences in sexual unions, and opportunity was afforded for the development of strong attachments. The permanence of these attachments was conditioned by the exigencies of the plantation system and the various types of social control within the world of the plantation.
>
> Within this world the slave mother held a strategic position and played a dominant role in the family groupings. The tie between the mother and her younger children had to be respected not only because of the dependence of the child upon her for survival but often because of her fierce attachment to her brood (Frazier 1948:360–361).

Herskovits and his colleagues sought survivals, syncretisms, and reinterpretations of Africanisms in many areas of culture. They were most successful in music, in dance, and in religion; they were least successful in economy and politics. Their most controversial assertions in the realm of domestic organization, as cited above, have little currency today, since structural and ecological emphases are now favored over historical ones. But Herskovits made a great contribution in opening up a whole area to serious inquiry. Indeed he established a tradition of scholarship in both the Caribbean and Africa, and a large number of students have followed him in working in the two regions. Mintz' assessment of Herskovits' *Life in a Haitian Valley* may serve as an evaluation of his Caribbean studies in general: "This is pioneering work . . . As ethnography, it does not meet the standards of modern field method, and it leaves many questions unanswered. As a ground-breaking anthropological study of a society previously either ignored or slandered by casual incompetents, it is of first importance" (Mintz 1964*b*:46).

During the early 1930s anthropologists and rural sociologists began to develop what came to be known as the community-study method, an approach to the study of complex civilizations. Redfield in Mexico, Arensberg in Ireland, the Lynds in the Midwest, and Warner in New England, to name only the leaders, worked in the rural areas and small towns of great nations, treating them as if they had the characteristics of the primitive bands and tribes usually associated with anthropological inquiry. Redfield's typology of communities, the "folk-urban continuum," provided a frame within which these rural villages could be located. It became clear that to know the culture of a nation, it was necessary to know the kinds of local expressions of culture which were contained within it. Julian Steward's monumental *The People of Puerto Rico* (1956) combined community study and typology with cultural ecology, isolating the major varieties of local organization on the island. He felt that these varieties or subcultures were determined by their commitment to different crops—tobacco, coffee, and sugar—and to concomittant different forms of production, land tenure, and distribution within the limits of a single large tradition:

> We selected municipalities exemplifying these principal types of farm production and sought to determine whether significant differences in the more important aspects of cultural behavior were associated with the type of production and with the individual's status and role within the community. In the field research, we sought to ascertain subcultural differences between certain classes or categories of rural people by analyzing their methods of making a living, family types, social relations, political and religious forms, practices and attitudes, varieties of recreation, and life values. We paid particular attention to differences associated with the individual's position in the community, whether as townsman or rural dweller, farm owner, sharecropper, or laborer, merchant, government employee, wage worker, and the like. The lifeways which distinguish the members of these different segments of rural society are presented as subcultures, as self-consistent patterns which prescribe the behavior of the local group of which the individual is a member (Steward: 2).

The constituent studies of Robert A. Manners, Sidney W. Mintz, Elena Padilla, and Eric R. Wolf established new standards for ethnographic documentation in the West Indies. The authors brought to prominence the plantation as a social form and the opposed implications of peasant and plantation systems of agriculture, which Ortiz (1947) had earlier called a counterpoint in Cuban history.

Edith Clarke's study (1957) of three rural Jamaican villages similarly combined the community-study method with cultural ecology, although her interests are less ambitious than those of Steward and his associates. The villages sampled—Sugartown, an estate-complex of landless cane cutters; Orange Grove, a community based on successful mixed farming on small to medium-sized plots, oriented to local markets; and Mocca, an impoverished village of subsistence cultivators—were selected to show the relationships between land tenure and varieties of mating and domestic organization. Clarke did not deny that slavery, nor even Africa, had a part to play in determining the kinds of alternatives available; rather, she said, within the limits drawn by history, the alternative selected may be understood in terms of variations in economy and community structure.

Clarke made liberal use of quantitative material in arguing her thesis. A quantitative sequential approach is found in the other two major studies of domestic organization in the Caribbean: Raymond T. Smith's *The Negro Family in British Guiana* (1956) and Michael G. Smith's *West Indian Family Structure* (1962). R. T. Smith shows that the several forms of household units coexisting in Guianese villages are actually at different stages of a developmental cycle. The limited role of lower-class adult males as husband-father is related by Smith to their marginal economic positions in the larger society. This is particularly the case on plantations, as shown in Clarke's presentation of Sugartown, for the domestic grouping does not assume corporate functions. Different from the peasant household, that of the plantation worker is totally divorced from economic productivity and distribution. The members of the plantation household individually contract to labor for wages; the members of a peasant household may collectively organize for planting and harvesting. The woman in a peasant household has special responsibility in overseeing the sale of the harvest. M. G. Smith's study also evidences, from a much more broadly drawn sample, developmental sequences of domestic organization. M. G. Smith compares households from Carriacou in the Grenadines, and from rural and urban areas in Grenada and Jamaica. He demonstrates that the organization of the family is a function of the conjugal pattern chosen by its head: extraresidential mating, coresidential mating or consensual cohabitation, and marriage. He shows further that not all of these patterns are available everywhere, and that a specific pattern is appropriate and sanctioned at a particular stage in the life cycle. I have found M. G. Smith's presentation tremendously useful, and the analysis of domestic organization in Chapter 5 relies upon it heavily.

The complex ethnic and racial character of many of the islands has occasioned studies of social stratification, of race relations, and of cultural pluralism. and has forced into the anthropological consciousness problems which were traditionally associated with sociology. Especially promising has been the extension of research from the large islands of the Greater Antilles and Trinidad, which had been studied for twenty years, to the smaller islands forming the arc of the eastern Caribbean. The work now going on and recently completed in the Virgin Islands, Montserrat, Dominica, the Dutch Windwards, Martinique, St. Lucia, the Grenadines, and Barbados, should provide the basis for genuinely comparative analyses. Much of the impetus for these studies stems from the establishment of the Institute for Social and Economic Research at the University of the West Indies, which with its journal *Social and Economic Studies* offers Caribbean social scientists a meeting ground for the exchange of ideas. More recently, research units have appeared in Puerto Rico, the Virgin Islands, Martinique, and elsewhere. Graduate students from West Indian, American, Canadian, and European Universities arrive in ever-increasing numbers to do field studies and add to the now rich corpus of Antillean research. From an area almost totally ignored by social scientists, the West Indies are now among the more carefully studied regions in the world. We hope that this ethnographic description and analysis of a peasant village in the French West Indies will make a contribution to the increased understanding of the region.

2

An Historical View

Precolonists

THE ABORIGINAL ARAWAK or Igneri Indians, known in the Lesser Antilles only through archeological remains, had probably been driven out of Martinique by the Island-Carib Indians before Columbus discovered the island (Rouse 1964). They may have fled from Martinique and other islands of the Lesser Antilles to the Greater Antilles, where they continued building large, inland villages based upon a highly productive combination of slash-and-burn and irrigation farming. The production of maize, manioc, and other crops beyond the subsistence needs of the farmers permitted the development of an elaborate system of social and political stratification. Arawak chiefs directed affairs, principally through the control of the distribution of surplus foods. They made judicial decisions that were enforced by an endogamous class of privileged persons who, by their associations with the chief and by their apparent exemption from horticultural labor, ranked above the mass of the people. Commoners and captive slaves worked the land, and were not permitted the special insignia, housing, food and titles of the aristocracy. Although polygyny was not restricted to the privileged class, the commoners usually could not afford to support several wives and their children. Despite the developed socioeconomic organization of the Arawaks, they were unimpressive soldiers, and were easily defeated by the fierce, egalitarian Caribs. The Caribs pursued them all the way to the Greater Antilles, but there, in Jamaica and Haiti, the inland location of Arawak villages provided a kind of defense against the maritime Carib raids, and Carib expansion ended when the Spanish occupied these islands. In Martinique it is the Caribs and not the original Arawaks whose influence is still felt.

For about twenty years following the French colonization of Martinique in 1635, relationships between the Caribs and the settlers were not actively hostile. The French cleared land on the Caribbean side of the island where there are sheltered harbors, and were separated by a spine of mountains from the Indians on the Atlantic side. Mid-seventeenth century maps show a formal division of the island with a western *terre des Français* and an eastern *terre des sauvages.* In Cardinal Richelieu's original plans for the colonization of the island was the order to instruct and convert the native population, and a number of the priests who were sent out to missionize the Indians wrote detailed descriptions of their culture and language.

West Indian Carib culture was a variant of the horticultural village culture that occupied most of the forests of lowland equatorial South America. Subsistence was based largely upon slash-and-burn cultivation of root crops (manioc, native taros, sweet potatoes), beans and maize. Fruit trees were also cultivated. The Island Carib differed from mainland tropical forest peoples by emphasizing salt-water fish in the diet and by the almost total lack of hunting. In contrast to the stratified Arawak, Carib society knew little status differentiation other than the dominant position of adult men. All men were warriors and derived prestige from individual acts of daring. Women captives had to serve the men and wait upon their husbands in the communal men's house. The Carib are supposed to have tortured and eaten their male victims, but their reputation for cannibalism may be exaggerated.

Following the death of Governor du Parquet in 1658 Carib-French relationships rapidly deteriorated, and the settlers organized a punitive expedition to rid the island entirely of Indians. In 1660 a treaty was signed in St. Kitts between the Indians and the French and English, in which the Caribs agreed to evacuate the islands for the exclusive occupation of St. Vincent and Dominica. Some must have remained in Martinique, however, to judge by the frequency of Carib names in eighteenth-century church records. Doubtless through intermating they slowly fused with the dominant population. Today there are no persons identifiable as Carib in Martinique, although many families proudly but undemonstrably claim some Carib ancestry.

There has been no systematic study of the influence of Indian culture in the French West Indies today, but there are obvious survivals in several areas. The most important is in subsistence crops. The *gros légumes* which form the base of rural nutrition include sweet potatoes, yams, and manioc which were farmed by the Indians, who taught the colonists the technique for removing poisonous prussic acid from the bitter manioc root and grinding the root into flour. Much of the characteristic Martinique handicraft also seems to be a Carib legacy, particularly in basketry, pottery, canoe making, and the traditional thatching of house roofs. Finally, Martiniquan vocabulary has been enriched by words of Indian provenience, such as *carbet* (men's house), *ajoupa* (shelter), *caimite,* and *papayer* (indigenous fruits).

French Colonization

The colonization of Martinique was part of Richelieu's plan to challenge the Spanish monopoly in the New World. The Cardinal supported the efforts of the Company of St. Christopher (later reorganized as the West India Company) to establish in the West Indies a French peasantry, which was to provide both food and soldiers for the protection of metropolitan interests. The company, composed of young men primarily from the west of France who had been seasoned in St. Kitts, settled Martinique in 1635. Most of the settlers came as indentured laborers, or *engagés,* who contracted to work three years in return for their passage and, at the end of the indenture term, 300 pounds of tobacco. The tobacco was used to acquire land, for the motivation of the *engagés* was to join the ranks of the planters. Individual landholdings were small. More than half the surface was devoted to raising vegetables and meat for local consumption; tobacco, indigo, cotton, and ginger were grown for export. During the early years following colonization, life was difficult for the *engagés,* who often lacked food, were ravaged by disease and, occasionally, menaced by the Indians. But the life of the *colon* was not much better, and frequently the planter and his indentured laborer lived together, worked side by side in the fields, and ate the same food.

Mixed-subsistence and tobacco farming on small holdings proved profitable during the first decades of settlement, and it was possible for an industrious *engagé* to acquire a successful farm. The introduction of sugarcane, or rather the industrial process of obtaining sugar from the cane, completely altered the system which had developed, for cane cultivation demanded a new use of land and labor. The small farm with its contract laborers gave way to the large plantation worked by African slaves. Capitalization of the estate, including slaves, land, and mill, precluded the further entry of *engagés* or even small *colons* into the ranks of the planters. By the end of the seventeenth century, so much land had been devoted to cane that Martinique became dependent upon importation to satisfy its own subsistence needs —a dependence which continues to the present day.

Neither the indentured laborers from France nor the indigenous Island-Carib could satisfy the enormous labor demands of the estates. The planters turned toward Africa, and within fifty years after the first settlers landed, the slave population was twice that of the European.

Under the plantation system, Martiniquan society was doubly stratified: by class and by color. The great landowners, government officials, professionals and clergymen were white; the agricultural laborers, servants, and artisans were Negro and mostly slaves. Yet shortly after the introduction of slavery a third group appeared, the freedmen, who were intermediate both in color and position. The illegitimate offspring of white masters and female slaves provided the largest source of freedmen. In the early days of slavery such children may have been born free. But when the king assumed possession of the island from the West India Company in 1674, children were accorded the status of their mothers, thus forcing the white fathers to pay the same head tax to the crown for their own children as for any other slave. The freed population increased regularly and by 1848, the year of general emancipation, it constituted a third of the 113,000 persons in Martinique.

Freedom did not mean equality. The Black Codes of 1685 officially equated the two concepts, but colored persons were discriminated against socially, politically, and economically. They were legally excluded from the civil service and the professions, although they could own land and, indeed, slaves. For instance, in the parish records of Covin for 1811, the priest wrote: "On June 15 I baptised Marie, born May 23, illegitimate daughter of Sophie, a Negro slave belonging to Pierre Macarie, a free Negro." Most freedmen became craftsmen (carpenters, cabinetmakers, bakers, etc.), but some bought or were given by their fathers small parcels of land in the highlands which, because of their steepness and distance from the mills, were unsuited for sugarcane. On these plots the freedmen practiced subsistence farming of vegetables and fruits, and sold their occasional surpluses to the lowland and coastal estates. We do not know how many there were nor the amount of land they worked, but the frequency of such highland place names as *Fonds Gens Libres* (Valley of the Freedmen) and *Rue Mulâtre* (Street of the Colored Men) attests to their importance.

The desire to be free motivated many slaves to run away, even though they courted imprisonment, mutilation, and death. These maroons, as they were called, fled to the mountainous interior that provided some refuge from the soldiers who sought them out. There they subsisted by raising vegetables on minuscule plots, by hunting, and by making charcoal, which was clandestinely sold to freedmen and plantation slaves, who resold it to exporters for shipment to Barbados, St. Kitts, and other islands that lacked forests. After 1833 when slavery ended in the British colonies, the maroons tried to reach neighboring St. Lucia and Dominica.

Since they frequently had white fathers and Negro mothers, the freedmen tended to be intermediate in physical characteristics. And since they were economically superior to the slaves, the term "*mulâtre*" came to signify both physiognomy and social position. Thus an impoverished white, called *petit blanc* in French and *béké goyave* in Creole, and a successful *noir* were both considered sociologically *mulâtre*. Among persons of color, much more subtle gradations were recognized, ostensibly based on ancestry but in fact determined by appearance. The steps from *blanc* to *noir* included *quarteron, métis, mulâtre, capre,* and *gryphe*. A *chabin* was any person of color with blond or red hair. Many of these terms are still used for white or Negro characteristics measured principally by skin color, hair form, and facial features. The epithet *nègre* is less a physical description than it is a reference to rural or old-fashioned beliefs and practices.

Among the objectives of the French Revolution was the termination of slavery and the political integration of the American colonies with the metropole. These liberal sentiments were never transcribed into action in Martinique where the slaveowners, opposed to the Revolution, encouraged a British occupation and maintenance of the former regime. The English remained in control until the Treaty of Amiens in 1802, and following Napoleon's accession to complete power the islands reverted to their prerevolutionary colonial status. The revolt of Toussaint l'Ouverture prevented the reversion in St. Domingue where the colonial aristocracy was overthrown and the Republic of Haiti established.

During the middle half of the nineteenth century slavery was abolished in the New World: 1833 for the British colonies; 1848 for the French; 1863 in the United States; 1886 in Cuba; and 1888 in Brazil. The causes of emancipation were many, and varied from place to place. In part it was due to humanistic agitation, in part to the rising costs of maintaining a labor force which had to be fed and housed throughout the year, although the productive months may have been few. But the principal cause everywhere was the competition for supremacy between the emerging industrial capitalism of the mills and cities and the allodial aristocracy of the colonial or rural estates. The industrial capitalists used emancipation as a weapon to destroy the planters. In Guadeloupe they succeeded. The planters, hard pressed by competition from the new beet sugar industry in France, did not survive emancipation, and their lands passed to the ownership of overseas corporations. In Martinique the former slave owners were able to continue in possession of the lands, although now they were forced to hire laborers. Today, the great estates and sugar mills in Martinique belong to descendants of the original owners and are frequently organized in the form of corporations.

To continue working on the same plantation for the same *patron* had little appeal to the now salaried cane cutter. Wherever they could the former slaves abandoned the estates, and moved into the hills to join peasant hamlets which had earlier been founded by the freedmen, the maroons, and an occasional impoverished white. Even the offer of a salary proved little enticement. The result was a labor shortage which brought about a reintroduction of the system of indentured labor. This time, however, nothing could induce the mainland French to accept these contracts. The recruiters had to look elsewhere. From 1852 to 1887 over 90,000 *engagés* came to the islands. Africa was the logical place to begin, and there are a few hamlets in the south of the island which claim to have been founded by these *congos* or postemancipation Africans. The vast majority came from Asia, particularly from India. The Chinese never numbered more than a thousand, and, in distinction to some of the islands where they form an ethnically and economically identifiable group, they too have been absorbed. Several families have Chinese surnames and may have members who have distinguishable features, but they do not otherwise differ from the bulk of the Martiniquans. Only the East Indians, descendants of the 10,000 who remained after the termination of this second attempt at indenture in 1887, constitute a self-consciously distinct element in the population. By face, occasionally by language, but primarily by endogamy and religion, the East Indians, or *coolies* as they continue to be called, maintain their separation. Concentrated in the north of the island, they still work in the sugar fields abandoned by the Negroes. Although individual East Indians have entered commerce and the professions, as a group they occupy the lowest economic level in the country. Their main distinction is their continued devotion to the worship of village deities, a persistence of the rural South Indian form of Hinduism practiced by their low-caste ancestors. Both in Martinique and in Guadeloupe they have built temples and propitiate their deities by shamanistic possession and animal sacrifice.

The Second Empire did not rescind emancipation; but it did identify its interests with those of the white planters, who continued to control the political as well as economic life of the colony. Dire predictions of economic failure and even massacres of the former masters proved false. The establishment of land-credit banks actually enabled the planters to improve their position by making it possible for them to build large steam-driven sugar factories (*usines*) processing enormous quantities of cane. During slavery each plantation had had its own animal-powered *sucrerie* and distillery. The new factories processed all the cane into sugar in much less time, with resultant savings in labor. Thus the rhythm of labor in the sugar fields and factories was six months of activity from January to June, and six months of forced unemployment. A few workers (*gens casés*) were housed on the estates to provide what little labor was needed during the dead period.

For twenty-two years following emancipation, the former slaves silently acquiesced to the situation of political and economic inferiority. Then the reestablishment of the Republic in 1870 triggered an uprising in the south of the island. Although it lasted only a few days and with apparently few fatalities, the more than forty plantations destroyed are evidence of the extent of the dissatisfaction with the status quo. There have been sporadic uprisings and strikes in the sugar fields from that time to the present as the workers have attempted to better their positions. The famous *biguine, Mama la grev bare mwê,* commemorates one of these strikes:

Mamâ la grev bare mwê	Mamma, I am blocked by the strike
M'sieur Michel pa le bai de francs	M'sieur Michel won't give two francs
Yo fe brule yô beke	They are burning a *béké*
Yo fe incende bitation yo	They are burning the plantation
Malgre tu sa yo fe yo	Despite all they are doing to them
M'sieur Michel pa le bai de francs	M'sieur Michel won't give two francs.

But while the economy of the island rested with the *békés,* the Third Republic concentrated, by universal franchise, whatever political power was delegated to the General Council in the hands of people of color.

The Council agitated for political integration with France, requesting that the legal codes of the metropole, and only those codes, be applied. These demands were heard throughout the seventy years of the Third Republic, and were silenced only by the Vichy regime during World War II, which restored the political supremacy of the white planters. Allied warships blockaded the island and prevented the exportation of sugar and rum and the importation of food. Widespread famine was averted only by doles of food from the United States. With the establishment of the Fourth Republic reaction to the deprivations of the war were immediate; both Martinique and Guadeloupe voted overwhelmingly Communist. In 1946 the Communist deputy, Aimé Césaire, forcefully presented the demand for assimilation to the now receptive National Assembly. Along with French Guiana in South America and Reunion in the Indian Ocean, the West Indian colonies were accorded the status of Overseas Departments, in principle equivalent to those in France. The Governor was replaced by a prefect appointed in Paris. Each island elects, by universal adult suffrage, three deputies and two senators to the national legislature.

The most immediate benefit of departmentalization was the application, with some modification, of the extensive social security system of France. *Assistance Médicale Gratuite* provides free medical and pharmaceutical care to most of the population; *Allocation Familiale* aids families of salaried persons; and *Assistance à la Famille* covers those not salaried, like agricultural tenants and small landowners.

West Indian social structure has frequently been described as a color-class pyramid: at the apex a white landed aristocracy, in the middle a colored middle and professional class, and at the base a black proletariat. In Martinique at least, color-class relationships are more complex and subtle and involve a delicate etiquette which is not readily discerned by the casual observer. In the first place a distinction must be made between economic and political power. Martiniquan economy is predicated upon the exportation of sugar and rum, bananas, and pineapples. All of the cane is processed in a dozen great factories belonging to white families. Forty-five percent of cultivated land is devoted to cane, most of which is grown on estates of at least 40 hectares apiece. In 1936, the last year for which such information is available, estates of 40 hectares and larger covered 75 percent of the land, but were controlled by less than 6 percent of the proprietors. In addition, all but two or three of the large distilleries are owned by these white families. Banana cultivation is more broadly distributed throughout the agricultural population, but increasingly, as the value of bananas has begun to challenge that of sugar as an export crop, the *békés* have taken land out of cane and substituted bananas, which today occupy 25 percent of all cultivated land. All export pineapple cultivation is on white-owned lands. More than 45 percent of all persons working for salaries or wages are employed in the cultivation and processing of these three crops.

The *blancs créoles* also dominate the import trade, although here, as in the distillation of rum, are found several colored families and an occasional metropolitan white. The *mulâtres* and the *métropolitains* are more commonly associated with the professional, governmental, and white-collar occupations. The former, largely excluded from effective access and exploitation of estate quality lands, have made use of the availability of good secondary school and university educations which France has provided in the West Indies. The eruption of Mt. Pelée in 1902 and the resultant destruction of the commercial center of St. Pierre abruptly killed many of the whites who had been the physicians, lawyers, civil servants, and secondary school professors, and accelerated the entry of colored Martiniquans. Many university-educated Martiniquans remain in France or find positions in the French overseas administrations. Martiniquans are especially prominent in the civil service in French-speaking Africa.

The metropolitan whites are in the civil service and in commerce. Almost all of them live in the capital city of Fort-de-France and its suburbs, except for the few, such as the *gendarmes,* who are assigned to rural areas. Both economically and socially the metropolitans are on a par with the colored middle class. They are not accorded the status of *békés* whose exclusiveness is reinforced by endogamy. Having heard of the colonial reputation and racial hierarchy in the island, a number of metropolitan whites arrive expecting to be accorded the deference they believe is due their color. They quickly learn, though, that their social position is determined by their occupation and by their birthplace. Marriage between colored Martiniquans of either sex and metropolitans is common, especially among those who were educated in France.

As there are middle-class *blancs* so are there middle-class *noirs*. These are persons who typically lack the economic benefits of demonstrable white ancestry and the social benefits of facial characteristics which approximate the Europeans, but who by virtue of their occupation and education are drawn up from the masses. Several have achieved prominence in politics where they may have an advantage with the electorate; in recent years, the left-wing parties have made racial appeals to the voters. Middle-class *noirs* also marry metropolitans, but less frequently than do the *mulâtres*.

Although the largest stores are owned by metropolitan and native whites and a few colored persons, much of the retail trade occurs in little shops owned and operated by Martiniquans of color and, especially in Fort-de-France, by a relatively endogamous group of North Africans and Southwest Asians generically referred to as Syrians. These grocery and dry-goods shops extend credit enabling poor people to buy food and clothing during the times of the year when employment and money are scarce.

The vast majority of the population is a rural proletariat, working in the fields and factories during the six months of the cane harvest, unemployed or underemployed for the remainder of the year. Most of the *noirs* are found in this group as are almost all of the East Indians. Although the application of social security benefits and the vigorous trade union of cane cutters has materially raised the standard of living of these workers in recent years, they are generally considered to occupy the lowest-status positions in the island, a sentiment derived from the continued equation of plantation labor with slavery.

As everywhere in the developing world, the city has a strong attraction for rural folk, and as everywhere, those who do leave the farms for the city have a difficult time finding work. For men, the major possibility is to become a *dockeur* or stevedore loading steamships with sacks of sugar and stems of bananas. For women, domestic service is a possibility: in 1961, more than 8000 women, about 25 percent of all women employed, were household servants. Of course some persons from the country do find work in shops and factories. Men may be apprentices to artisans, or become truck drivers and chauffeurs. Despite the attempt of the government to expand employment, however, the chances of finding a job are declining as the population expands more rapidly than the economy. Between 1954 and 1961 the population increased from 239,000 to 290,000, about 3 percent per year. Over 42 percent of the population is less than fifteen years old.

The rural population includes two other groups. Scattered along the coasts are little villages of fishermen, who go out in small open-plank canoes with nets to provide fish for local markets. Although recently many fishermen have acquired outboard motors, fishing remains slightly developed and provides only a small amount of the food consumed on the island. Indeed, people eat more dried and salted cod imported from Scandinavia and St. Pierre and Miquelon than locally caught fresh fish. Peasant villagers in the hills, still raising fruits and vegetables for household consumption and for sale in the urban markets, form the other part of the rural population. Founded as we have seen by freedmen and runaway slaves, and receiving an influx of former slaves in the mid-nineteenth century, these communities form an important part of the life of the island. They have, often with difficulty, maintained an independence from the estates for a hundred years, but their ability to survive much longer is threatened by the demographic pressures of a rapidly expanding population on limited land resources and by the increased importation of metropolitan vegetables which successfully compete in price with those grown locally. A description and analysis of one of these villages is the task of this book.

3

The Village

MORNE-PAYSAN is a village some 5 kilometers inland and 380 meters above the coastal town of Covin. The Caribbean shore from Covin to Case Pilote was the area of original settlement in Martinique, and was the first part of the island to be planted in sugarcane. The estates avoided the mountainous Pitons du Covin, because the land was too broken for large-scale cane cultivation. Thus the area was settled by freed and runaway slaves, and later by some white planters who raised coffee, cacao, and small amounts of cane for rum.

The earliest official mention of Morne-Paysan reports the baptism, in 1796, of an illegitimate son born to Bernardine, a free woman of color who lived in the hamlet. By 1850 the population had reached 1400 persons as the emancipated slaves from the coast moved up into the hills. At least thirty-six family names in Morne-Paysan today are inscribed in the *Registre des Individualités,* the official record of surnames chosen in 1848. The Covin parish priest, recognizing the large population in the hills, pressured for the construction of a church in Morne-Paysan; by 1872 there was a presbytery and, shortly after, a cemetery. Before the end of the nineteenth century there were primary schools and an office of the *Etat civil.* the state registry of birth, recognition and legitimation, marriage, and death.

But it was not until 1947 that the inhabitants successfully petitioned for separation from Covin, which had been responsible for its administration since the eighteenth century. The villagers argued that their special needs as small farmers were inadequately represented in a town whose economy was based upon the plantation and the sea. Morne-Paysan was granted the legal status of *commune* with its own mayor and municipal council.

Nestled in the foothills of the almost impossibly steep Pitons du Covin, with perhaps the most beautiful scenery in all of Martinique and certainly the most comfortable climate, Morne-Paysan is nevertheless an isolated commune. Thousands of tourists taxi each year up the littoral from Fort-de-France to the ruins of St. Pierre left by the catastrophe of 1902, and pass within 3 kilometers of Morne-Paysan, yet they never visit it. The only indication of the village is a sign on a side road, for Morne-Paysan is nowhere visible from the littoral. Two very poor roads connect it to the littoral; one, of about 3 kilometers, meets the littoral at a relatively high point, up away from the sea. The other connects Morne-Paysan with Covin. These are the only roads in or out of the village. No traffic passes through Morne-Paysan on its way to someplace else.

Because of the high Pitons behind it, Morne-Paysan enjoys a much greater rainfall each year than the coastal line of the island. Thus, during the dry season, a visitor walking the 3 kilometers from the littoral climbs from an arid, parched, brown and yellow countryside, up a steep, twisty, rutty road, to find himself sud-

The bourg, *showing the church, the main street, and the surrounding Pitons du Covin.*

denly confronting a deep green valley, so lush by comparison, so refreshing and so different, that he turns to look back at the parched plain he has just left. The Caribbean Sea and the dry coastline are completely out of sight, and the visitor may feel almost dizzy as he searches for a single horizontal line. The horizon is jagged. The crazy ups and downs of the hills and valleys are criss-crossed with odd-shaped little plots, meandering paths, and little huts placed in no obvious relation to each other. Some of the hilltops are plain, green meadows with cows pasturing there. The visitor is amazed simultaneously by the steepness of the terrain, the vivid and deep green of the vegetation, the refreshing cool air, and the pervading quiet.

After two or three more twists in the road, he finds himself in the *bourg.* The church dominates the *bourg,* as well as the whole commune, for it can be seen and its bells heard in all the outlying *quartiers.* The simple, white-plaster church rises up above the street on the right, approached by wide steps. This is the center of town. The road widens in front of the church, and it is here that the two buses load and unload. Across from the church is a small, square, yellow wooden structure, labeled "PTT" (post, telephone, and telegraph). Just behind is a similar structure, the clinic. All the accoutrements of the modern state are strung out along this road, which is the ridge of a steep hill: boys' and girls' schools, police station, town hall, the presbytery behind the church, stores, bars, houses, and, a little further along, the cemetery. There is no plaza or public square around which these public structures and larger stores and bars are concentrated; they are lined up on the ridge. Behind this row of buildings along the road is another row, just a few meters distant, but hidden because of the foliage-covered escarpment. Behind these are the fields, and further on, other aggregations of house and fields, the *quartiers*. In the *bourg,* wherever two buildings are separated by a strip of land not used as a path, no matter how narrow, that strip is cultivated or given to small animals. Every yard has rabbit hutches, a pig or two, and some chickens, as well as several fruit trees. Goats and sheep are staked in the grass along the street and chickens peck freely. Even the lands around the church and town hall are farmed.

Along the street in the *bourg* there are some half-dozen general stores in which the people buy the imported goods they need: soap, matches, kerosene, cooking oil, salt cod, salt, rice, bread, and tobacco. The stores also sell cloth, shoes, school supplies, tools, pots and pans, kerosene burners, sewing supplies, pitchfork tines, hoe blades, and the like. They also stock luxury food items like canned goods, wine, and imported potatoes. Some of these stores are licensed to serve rum on the premises and have a few tables and chairs. There are also several bars not associated with stores. In every bar and shop there is a sign prominently announcing that "credit is not extended in order not to lose friends"; in fact, most trade is on credit. Each customer has a notebook in which his purchases are recorded. Although he is supposed to settle accounts monthly, shopkeepers do not pressure for payment during the dry season when there is little money in the village. Eventually accounts must be paid or the shopkeeper brings suit in court. Recourse to the courts is a source of considerable tension in the community and a cause of serious hostility between the shopkeepers and their clientele.

About 80 percent of the villagers do not live in the *bourg,* but reside in dispersed neighborhoods of from about five to thirty households each. Most of these *quartiers* were single properties in the nineteenth century which, after two or three generations of fragmenting inheritance, now are divided into many small holdings. Instead of the neat rows of houses flanking the street that we find in the *bourg,* each house in the *quartier* is on its own piece of land, usually surrounded by a hedge, and frequently at some distance from the main paths. Since it is often necessary to cross land belonging to someone else in order to reach one's own plot, one continually hears the cry, *"permission à pénétrer?"* ("may I enter?") as people move about. Until recently there were no roads opening the *quartiers* to ordinary automobiles; other than the mayor's jeep, people and produce moved by foot or by donkey.

Most rural houses are wattle-and-daub structures calles *cases* or *gaulettes.* Bamboo poles are set into the ground every 8 to 10 inches to a height of about 7 feet, forming a square from 10 to 15 feet on a side. Horizontal strips of bamboo are tied with vines on both sides of the vertical poles. Coarsely chopped sugarcane leaves are mixed with mud, and the resultant mortar-like substance is forced into the interstices in the walls. After it dries, the walls are plastered inside and out, but after one or two rainy seasons the plaster begins to chip away. Most of the houses have at least partially exposed walls. The roof is made either of thatch from sugarcane leaves laid on a wooden frame or, increasingly, of corrugated galvanized iron. People speak nostalgically of the declining use of thatch, arguing that it is cooler and "better for the health." But metal roofs last longer, give better protection against the rain, and are more modern (*civilisés*).

The floors are left earthen, tramped down to be smooth and hard. Sometimes there is but a single room in the *case* in which the entire family sleeps and stores its important possessions. Usually they divide the house with a rough wooden partition into a parlor and a bedroom. In such cases each room may have a separate door to the outside and a separate wooden-shuttered window. The preferred division of a house into two rooms is reinforced by the expectation that each partner on establishing a household is responsible for furnishing one of the rooms.

Food is prepared outside in a kitchen, separate from the house. It is a simple wattle-and-daub shed, containing a small charcoal-burning oven, a water basin, a few pots and pans, and a screened chest. Some of the people cook with kerosene primus stoves. The kitchen is kept separate to keep vermin away from the house.

Furnishings are usually very crude and simple. The poorest people have just a slat bed with a straw-stuffed mattress, one or two benches, and a rough table. The interior walls are covered with magazine illustrations or just plain newspaper. No matter how impoverished, however, every home has a number of religious decorations such as the Sacred Heart of Jesus, a picture of the Virgin, and a crucifix. There is also frequently a reproduction of Millet's "Gleaners," and occasionally a framed picture of De Gaulle. Then there are many photographs of relatives, especially young men in uniform. A single kerosene lamp provides all the illumination at night, and during the day the single window admits little light.

About 12 percent of the houses have piped in water and about 11 percent have electricity; almost all of these are in the *bourg*. Most of the people who live in the *bourg* get their water from public stands along the street; more than half the people of the commune receive water from the several narrow streams which cut through the region. These streams or *rivières* are the sole source of drinking water in the rural *quartiers*, and are places where women and girls meet to do their laundry. Because of their all-purpose use, they have become contaminated with snails which host the blood fluke (*Schistosoma mansoni*), causing a parasitic disease endemic in the village and throughout northern Martinique. Sanitation is rudimentary. A chamber pot is kept in the house and emptied in an open cesspool shared by several families.

A few of the homes in the *quartiers* and many in the *bourg* are much larger stone and wooden houses with tiled roofs. A number of these date from the mid-nineteenth century and once were the residences of prosperous farmers. They were elaborately furnished with the massive mahogany and marble cabinetry for which

Martinique was famous. As a consequence of the division of property every generation, some of these armoires and tables now furnish the rural *cases.* In a wattle-and-daub hut it is not uncommon to be offered drinks in hand-cut crystal goblets from Limoges. Occasionally persons from the city comb the countryside for antique Martiniquan furniture which now competes with Scandinavian modern among sophisticated urbanites.

The house is surrounded by a small semienclosed yard. Except when it rains, all meals are eaten here, guests are received, and children play. The woman keeps the yard scrupulously clean, sweeping several times a day with a twig broom. The yard is usually filled with animals: the chicken coop and rabbit hutches are there and there is usually a dog who informally attaches himself to the family and feeds himself from whatever waste is available. Several fruit trees, like breadfruit, mango, and orange, are planted in the yard, and there are often several guava trees which grow wild. Many families devote a portion of the yard to a small herb garden for kitchen spice and medicinal use.

At the end of the path from the house to the road or at the juncture of two roads there is often a small masonry replica of a house containing religious statues. These *chapelles* are built in honor of a saint by a grateful or petitioning villager. Most of them are very old, having been there longer than the memories of the present inhabitants of the house. Each evening candles or an oil lamp are lit inside, just as one is lit before the crucifix or Sacred Heart in the house, and often a vase of fresh flowers is placed inside. A number of the *chapelles* have a collection box attached in which the passersby used to be invited to make a contribution to pay for a mass at the church. While this custom is no longer practiced, a few families place a collection plate near the little Nativity scene which decorates the house at Christmas and use the contributions to purchase new figures for the following years. A massive crucifix often towers over a major intersection.

In the *quartiers* there are few large stores and bars. Rather there are tiny shops, usually in a room attached to the house, in which rum is sold, and sometimes bread, soap, matches, and a few other items. Such *débits de la régie* are part-time or secondary enterprises, usually managed by a woman. They are important points of congregation in the countryside, as men drop by for a drink, but they rarely provide any substantial income for their owners. Credit is extended here too, but on an informal basis, without written records.

Village children play soccer in the schoolyard and on the unpaved street in the *bourg,* kicking a ball, or an orange, or even a coconut, with bare feet. But while soccer is clearly the national sport and the best Martiniquan teams compete on other Caribbean islands and have hosted teams from Europe, the passions of adult men in the countryside run rather to fighting cocks. There are two arenas in Morne-Paysan consisting of three or four tiers of wooden benches surrounding an open space. There is not enough money in the village to support regular contests, and these *pits* are used primarily for training the birds. Then on Sunday during the gaming season groups of men go where the *pits* draw players from great distances and where their own cocks are less well known. At one of these large arenas several hundred dollars is commonly bet on the outcome of these contests which may last but a few seconds, and I have seen as much as a thousand dollars placed on a particularly famous bird or trainer.

The occupational structure of this peasant village is deceptively simple. Most people farm. Some farmers own large pieces of land, some own small plots, and some are landless. All peasants operate in a monetarized economy and try to provide for their needs by selling vegetables and fruits in the market as discussed in the next chapter. They frequently develop subsidiary skills which can be converted to cash to supplement the income from their plots. Thus remunerative roles in Morne-Paysan may be divided into full-time or primary occupations, whose players may own land but do not themselves cultivate, and part-time or secondary occupations of peasant farmers.

Some of the full-time occupations are: boys' school director, girls' school director, teacher, post and telephone office clerk, postman, forest ranger, town clerk, watermain repairman, policeman, market-seller (*revendeuse*), nurse, priest, bus driver, mason, large shopkeeper, large-shop clerk, *pension* (hotel) manager, and school janitor.

Some of the part-time occupations are: apprentice postman, midwife, bell-ringer, sacristan, road-gang worker, town hall janitor, truck driver, cab driver, bus driver's helper, apprentice mason, carpenter, cobbler, seamstress, baker, butcher, small shopkeeper, barmaid, barber, maid, gamecock trainer, flower-seller, fish-seller, wholesale milk merchant, retail milk merchant, straw-hat maker, and farm laborer.

An example of typical complexity is Jean Félix, who is a tenant on his father's land. His wife runs a shop and bar in their home. She is also a seamstress, specializing in white dresses for First Communion made from cloth sold in her own shop. Félix's half-share of the harvest is usually consigned to a professional seller who has a stall in the market in Fort-de-France. From time to time, however, when market prices are high, Mme. Félix rents a place in the market for herself. On these days, Félix stays home to run the shop and bar and to watch over their ten children, and repairs shoes. He is active in town politics on the mayor's side and is a municipal counsellor. This is not a paid position, but by virtue of his association with the mayor he is sometimes hired to supervise public activities such as road work and village celebrations. Finally he earns money as clerk of the new agricultural credit association.

In classical economic terms the class structure of Morne-Paysan would have the large landowners, the big-shop keepers, and perhaps the school directors at the top, and the landless laborers at the bottom. But within the community, these economically defined strata do not form self-conscious groups with a high degree of internal association. As far as the general society is concerned an inhabitant of Morne-Paysan is a small landholder, a peasant. None of the villagers, even the two large landowners who are of unmixed European ancestry, is considered a member of the *béké* elite. Within the village, prestige ranking is more nearly related to education, physical appearance, and personal characteristics than it is to wealth. An ideal person to be esteemed is one who is generous in relation to his means, religious without being self-righteous, hard working, educated without being a snob, and meets his obligations to family, friends, godchildren, and relatives.

Kinship extensions obscure the class structure: almost everyone in the village is related to everyone else. None of the large landowning families is without impoverished relatives. The obligations and reciprocal behavior demanded by kinship militate against the exercise of power and superordination of a strict class structure.

There is no residential segregation in the village. Wealthier people live in more substantial homes and are more likely to have water and electricity. But the house next door may be the mud-and-thatch hut of a landless cultivator. Then there are several large landholders whose homes are little better than these *cases en terre* or *gaulettes,* as there are poor people who have inherited impressive homes. There is even little distinction in dress. Men wear cotton pants, shirts, and large straw hats. Old women wear ankle-length dresses and a kerchief around the head. Younger women wear shorter cotton dresses. Both men and women are frequently shoeless, although some men wear rubber boots in the fields. Schoolteachers and civil servants are always well dressed, the men with shirt, tie and jacket, and the women in stylish clothes, high heels, and an umbrella.

Large landowners have potential power for they can refuse to rent their land to tenants. But this power is rarely invoked. Most tenancies have lasted for many years, and the relationship may pass to the descendants of the owner and the renter. As long as the tenant maintains the productivity of the land, he is not dispossessed. Tensions arise, especially at the division of the harvest, but claims of kinship can often be invoked to resolve them. Relatives are not supposed to haggle with each other, and within the village there is an expectation that the more affluent should make the major concessions.

In the next chapter we shall examine the economy of the highland peasantry in detail.

4

The Fields

WEST INDIAN ECONOMIES are based upon the production of one or a few crops and their exportation to markets overseas. In Martinique these crops are sugar, bananas, and pineapples, grown on large plantations and shipped in bulk to French ports. Since almost all revenues are derived from this trade, the government encourages its development with supported prices, agricultural experts, transportation facilitation, and loans. The economy of the highland peasants is also based upon agriculture, but instead of producing for foreign markets, the farmer in Morne-Paysan raises food for his own family's consumption and for sale in domestic markets. From time to time he may devote a portion or, rarely, most of his fields to a cash crop for export, gambling the possibility of higher returns against financial disaster; for if either the crop fails due to drought or hurricane, or the overseas price is too low, he will have neither food to eat nor cash to pay for his fields and the needs of his household. During the late nineteenth century there was a brief boom in coffee and cacao, which were profitably grown on small holdings, and the farmers were able to neglect subsistence production. As we have seen, tobacco was similarly grown in the mid-seventeenth century. Since the end of World War II, many peasants have put at least part of their fields in bananas, selling them through a cooperative run by the mayor.

Agricultural Crops and Rhythms

Annual rounds of agricultural work throughout the world vary with the cycle of seasonal changes. In temperate climates the major seasonal change has to do with temperature. In Martinique, as in most of the tropical and subtropical world, the principal variable is rainfall, while variations in temperature are secondary. The people divide the year into four seasons of about equal length:

1. *Le Carême*—the dry season, usually from February through April,

named after Lent which comes within this period. Rain seldom falls during *carême,* and there is little work in the fields.

2. *Le Renouveau*—the hot season, from May through July, when the rains begin to fall. During this season the *canicule* (dog days) may occur, in which a few dry days of very hot sunshine burn the young plants whose growth was encouraged by the rains.

3. *L'Hivernage*—the season of heavy rains and hurricanes, from August through October.

4. *Saison Fraîche*—the cool season from November through January, divided into *avant,* the rainy part before Christmas, and *après,* when the rains decline.

It is unusual of course for the seasons to arrive and depart exactly on schedule. The farmer can take normal variations in stride, but exceptionally early or late rains may be disastrous. In 1958, for example, there was no rain from the middle of December to the end of May, and all planting was retarded. Then the rains came so suddenly and with such strength that much soil was lost because there were no roots to hold it down. For the rest of the year, the villagers were forced to purchase large quantities of imported foods, mortgaging future harvests for credit.

The relationship between agricultural rhythms and seasonal variations is complex. It has to do in part with gross climatic demands such as rainfall and temperature, with differences in the nature of the fields (such as quality of soil, slope), whether the plant is grown for household consumption or for the market in which case the farmer might attempt to harvest when the supply is low and the price is high, and upon such customs as observing the phases of the moon. Several planters claim to follow advice on calendars printed in France and distributed as advertising in Martinique. These calendars list saints' days, phases of the moon, and predictions about the weather in Europe.

The peasant's primary productive goals are to provide food for himself and family and for sale in local markets. The receipts from the market are used to acquire necessities which he cannot produce himself (that is, cooking oil, cloth, hoe blades), to pay his rents and taxes, and to cover himself in emergencies. He also needs cash to entertain himself and his friends, to travel to the city, and to contribute to the activities of his church, political party, and village. His technique in Morne-Paysan is to plant a number of crops which mature in different cycles in order to have at least some foods for table and sale trickling in throughout most of the year.

Large tubers, called *gros légumes,* form the basic diet of most Martiniquans, and are listed below.

1. Yams or *ignames* (*Dioscorea* spp.), originally from Asia, were introduced in the early colonial period. They are typically planted during *carême,* with a first harvest in seven months and a second after twelve months. Often *choux caraibe* (see below) is planted in the same pits about a month after the yams. When kept dry, yams will keep for several months after the harvest. Some farmers suggest planting the variety *igname portugaise* (*D. rotundata* Poir) within three days of the first quarter of the moon; harvesting them during the last quarter is then supposed

Sowing a field which has been prepared by hoeing against the slope. Note the deep ditch which is used as a path and also to allow water to run off.

to result in a small number of heavy plants, and harvesting during the full moon, in a large number of small plants. The average plant weighs less than 10 pounds, but some have been reported as heavy as 80 pounds.

2. Taros include both the indigenous *choux caraibe* (*Xanthosoma sagittifolium* /L./ Schott) and imported *choux de chine* (*Colocasia antiquorum* Schott). The former is planted during the late dry season or early rains and harvested within six to ten months. They are often intercropped with yams, taking advantage of the manured pits. *Choux de chine* may be planted throughout the year, except during *carême,* and is harvested in six to twelve months.

3. Bitter and sweet manioc (*Manihot utilissima* Pohl) are planted during the early rainy season, usually alone but occasionally with other plants like tomatoes. The harvest may begin within eight months, but since the plant keeps well in the ground, the harvest may continue up to two years after planting. (This unusual storage ability of the plant and the flour ground from it help account for its rapid diffusion throughout the tropical world following its post-Columbian discovery in America.) Up to the middle of the nineteenth century in Martinique manioc was grown and processed on a commercial basis for export.

Manioc planting requires elaborate preparation of the fields in parallel rows of mounds, carefully arranged by hoe. Six-inch pieces of stalk are cut and examined to see that the small protuberances are pointed upward towards the top of the soil, then inserted obliquely in the mound and covered entirely with earth. Farmers say that if they are planted vertically, an elaborate root system develops which makes it very difficult to harvest.

Processing of bitter manioc involves removing toxic quantities of prussic acid. Although the equipment has changed some since Island-Carib times, the principles of treatment are the same. Plants are peeled and washed and brought to a mill for grating. There are about a half-dozen of these mills in the village, whose owners rent their use for 10 percent of the flour. The grater is a cylindrical piece of copper with a surface roughened by punched holes. This is connected by a belt to a wheel turned by two men. The roots are pushed against the turning cylinder and the gratings collected underneath. Some of the liquid is withdrawn and filtered through a piece of cloth to be used as laundry starch. When all the roots are grated they are placed in burlap sacks and pressed. The press is a long pole inserted in a concrete stanchion and forced down upon the sack of manioc, compressing the pulp and removing the poisonous juice. When dry the pressed flour is heated on a large metal plate over an oven. This may eliminate any lingering poison. Much of the flour is made into round flat cakes called *cassave* by adding lime juice, sugar, and spices. When only a small amount of manioc is made into flour a simple hand grater, a flat piece of metal into which sharp holes have been gouged and mounted on a board, is used.

4. Sweet potatoes or *patate douce* (*Ipomoea batatas* Poir), like manioc, are a native American crop. They are planted in mounds during the rainy season and may be harvested in three to six months.

5. Breadfruit or *fruit-à-pain* (*Artocarpus incisa* L.) is considered one of the *gros légumes,* although it is a tree crop. Introduced in the Caribbean from Tahiti by Captain Bligh at the end of the 18th century, breadfruit is the most important food of the poorest people in Martinique; to describe a man's diet as being predominantly breadfruit is sufficient in Martinique to indicate his poverty. The tree bears these fruits weighing between 2 and 4 pounds throughout the year, but especially during *l'hivernage.*

Morne-Paysan is noted in the island for the cultivation of the smaller vegetables (*légumes* and *salades*). The early European colonists introduced the eggplant, carrot, cabbage, maize, onion, turnip, tomato, lettuce, cucumber, and radish. Most of these can be planted at any time and mature within two to four months. Thus several plantings are possible within the year. Almost any combination of these may be intercropped, although lettuce is usually first planted in manured boxes and then transplanted after about a month.

Bananas are the only export crop of importance in Morne-Paysan, since there is little market for coffee and cacao, and pineapples are just beginning in that area. Bananas are planted in August, and harvested before the following *hivernage* to prevent loss of the crop from the strong rains and hurricanes which uproot the top-heavy trees. The stems are brought to a central shelter where they are weighed, padded, and wrapped in paper or plastic. From there they are trucked to the docks in the city and loaded on boats for shipment to Europe. Although the value of bananas as an export now rivals that of sugar, the fraction left to the small producer is not very great. The average price of a kilogram in France is about 40 cents retail and 28 cents wholesale. The cost of shipment, including wrapping, customs, stevedores' fees, and transportation is 12 cents and the wholesaler's profit is 10 cents, leaving 6 cents to the planter. From this he must pay for the land, fertilizer, and insecticides. The gross receipts from an hectare of bananas (30,000 kg) is about $1800. Less than 50 percent of the holdings total as much as an hectare, and few small planters dare risk more than a fraction of their lands to a crop so vulnerable to the weather and to price changes in remote markets.

The other arborous crops are not exported. Most important of these are the many varieties of mangoes (*Mangifera indica* L.), called *julie, divine, d'or,* etc., avocado or *zaboca* (*Persea gratissima*), the citrus group (grapefruit, called *chadeque* or *fruit défendu,* orange, mandarine, lime, etc.), coconut (*Cocos nucifera*), and papaya (*Carica papaya* L.). Some others are the custard-apple or *corossol* (*Annona muricata* L.) and *pomme cannelle* (*A. squamosa* L.), the Indian almond or *amande* (*Terminalia catappa* L.), the indigenous *caimite* (*Chrysophyllum cainito* L.), the self-propagating group of quavas or *goyave* (*Psidium* spp.), the *quénette* (*Melicocca bijuga* L.), *pomme cythère* (*Spondias dulcis*), and *sapotille* (*Achras sapota* L.). Most of these begin to ripen during *hivernage* and continue until about December.

Spices and medicinal herbs are grown near the house. Martiniquan food is served highly flavored with hot peppers, called *piment* (*Capsicum* spp.), and other seasonings. Most women grow some garlic and shallots around the house, and many raise ginger or *gingembre* (*Zingiber officinale* Rose), gombo (*Hibiscus esculentus* L.), and turmeric or *safran* (*Curcuma longa* L.). Watercress is gathered wild along the banks of streams, and the heart of certain palm trees, like *choux palmiste* (*Oreodoxa oleracea* Mart. and *O. regia* Kth.), is used in salads. (Some medicinal plants and their uses are described in Chapter 7.)

Every household has some chickens, a goat or two, and a pig. Many also have rabbits, ducks, pigeons, and some sheep. The fowl are permitted to scratch freely and occasion disputes between neighbors when they get into freshly seeded fields. Goats and sheep are staked along the road or in fallow fields, but they too sometimes break away. Thus one sees crudely lettered signs in the country admonishing "Neighbors, tie your animals!" Rabbits have to be fed in their warrens, and one of the first economic tasks given to children is the gathering of vines and weeds to bring to the animals. During times when the market is flooded with carrots some farmers feed them to rabbits.

The ideal for every small cultivator is to have some cows. Asked what are the minimum conditions which provide security for a couple with five or six children, several villagers independently responded: one hectare in cultivation, one in pasturage, and one fallow. In the pastures they would place four milk cows, four calves, and four juveniles. In fact, over 450 hectares, more than 50 percent of all productive land in the village, is in pasturage. This is a recent development, and one which has serious consequences for the share farmers, since it removes land from tenancy. We shall return to this below.

There is no mechanization of peasant agriculture in Morne-Paysan, and there is no plough. Some people ride horses, mules, and donkeys, and use them for carrying the crops from the fields to the *bourg,* but they are not used for traction. Fields are prepared, weeded, and harvested with the aid of a long-handled hoe, a spade, and a pitchfork. Only the blades and tines are purchased ready-made, while the handles are made in the village. In addition to these, every man and many women carry a machete which, although primarily a cutting tool, may in fact be a substitute for all the others. The machete is an almost constant appendage to a man's costume.

Before planting, fields must be cleared. Sometimes the growth and stubble are burnt off, but usually they are simply cut and hoed under the soil. The duration of the fallow-planting cycle depends upon the quality of the soil, the kinds of plants grown, and the amount of land available. The average is four or five years of planting, rotating through the entire inventory of crops, and a fallow period of no more than four years. Even fallow land is used productively, for animals are pastured on the unplanted fields. A landless man may request permission to stake his cows or goats on another's fallow fields, and expect it to be granted. There is no payment but an exchange of manure for grazing land. We found only one villager who did not want to lend his land for pasture, and to avoid being asked, he regularly cleared his fallow fields of all growth. It is interesting that he preferred to expend energy in making his land unattractive for grazing instead of merely denying access to it. He was the only small cultivator who did not participate in labor-exchange groups, and used his military pension to hire day workers when needed.

Each field is clearly marked off by paths or a row of trees and bushes. The extreme steepness, limited tree cover and overplanting for more than one hundred years have resulted in serious erosion in many parts of the village. To minimize soil loss during the rainy season, most fields are contour-hoed. The specific preparation of the land depends on the plants to be grown.

For the *gros légumes,* foot-deep pits are dug in the furrows and then filled almost to the top with a mixture of manure, topsoil, and vegetation. Stakes are provided to keep the yam vines off the ground, and trellises built for the eggplant-like *christophine* (*Sechium edule* Sw.). Since the fields are intercropped and the plants mature at different times, there is continual planting, weeding, and harvesting most of the year.

Holdings and Tenure

Morne-Paysan has proportionately the largest agricultural population (62 percent of adult males) of any of the thirty-four communes in Martinique. Yet it has the smallest percentage of landless agricultural wage earners (11 percent), other than the capital city and its suburbs. This reflects the absence of sugar and large-scale banana plantations in the village. Typical holdings are very small. As the following table shows, half are less than 1 hectare each, and half of these are less than 100 square meters! Many holdings are too small to permit profitable exploitation, or to provide more than a fraction of the owner's needs.

Ideally, land is owned by an individual. Upon his or her death the heirs hire a land surveyor who "subjects the land to a friendly division." The Napoleonic code of inheritance requires that each child, male and female, inherit equally. The only exception is that illegitimate but recognized children (*enfants reconnus*) have fractional shares, the amount depending on the number of legitimate children. Illegitimate children (*enfants naturels*) have no rights in inheritance. The land surveyor draws up maps clearly showing the limits of the new properties, and these are recorded and filed along with the payment of certain taxes at the office of a notary. At these occasions some of the heirs, especially those who are not resident in the village, may sell their shares to the others or to outsiders.

It frequently happens, however, that the heirs do not immediately divide the inheritance. It may be that some of them live too far away, or are unwilling to accept the judgment of the surveyor. In such instances the land is kept undivided and an informal agreement is reached on how the land is to be farmed. One of them may agree to farm the whole piece and share the market proceeds with the others.

TABLE 2

LAND DISTRIBUTION IN MORNE-PAYSAN

Size of Holding (ha)	Number of Holdings	Percent of Total Holdings	Total Size (ha)	Percent of Total Area	Mean Size (ha)
less than 0.01	38	25.5	0.1905	0.02	0.0050
0.01 to 0.9	37	24.8	5.7394	0.66	0.1551
1 to 2.9	7	4.7	14.9891	1.72	2.1413
3 to 9.9	42	28.2	211.3661	24.25	5.0325
10 to 19.9	15	10.1	230.4730	26.44	15.3649
20 to 39.9	5	3.4	128.7020	14.77	25.7404
40 to 59.9	3	2.0	147.5225	16.93	49.1741
60+	2	1.3	132.5800	15.21	66.2900
TOTAL	149	100.0	871.5626*	100.00	5.8494

* Excluded are 210 hectares of state forest and .9 hectare of land owned by the commune.

Or they may decide to rent it outright to strangers. In any case it becomes increasingly difficult to come to a final decision as the primary heirs move away or die and have children and grandchildren who now have claims. In the following chapter, we shall examine the history of land division in a *quartier*.

Since agriculture is not mechanized, and there is a limit to the amount that an individual can work, the owners of large holdings who are interested in vegetable farming must either hire laborers or section the land and rent it out. Rented land is either for share (called locally *colonage*) or for cash (called *métayage*). *Colonage* is the most common form of tenancy, preferred by the tenant because he is not committed to paying a fixed amount. The *colon* agrees to provide the owner with either half the crop (in which case the system is called *moitié-moitié*) or a third (called *tiers*). At harvest the tenant either sets aside the owner's portion, occasionally under supervision, or he markets the entire crop and gives the owner his share in cash. Usually the tenant decides what crops he will plant and when they will be harvested, although some owners insist upon certain ones. Except for bananas where the owner may assume some of the expenses of fertilizer and insecticides, all the costs of cultivation are borne by the tenant.

Colonage extends to animals as well. For example, the owner of a cow may lend it to someone who can look after it and provide it with pasture. The tenant keeps the milk and shares equally in any progeny. When we first moved into the village a neighbor gave us two infant goats; at the end of the year, having cared for them, we were to keep one and return the other.

The fields. Individual holdings are often separated by coconut palm, banana, mango, and other trees.

The system of *colonage* provides an alternative to wage labor and a feasible ratio of land size to the labor force. It has clear disadvantages, for the tenant has no security in the land and will seldom make any improvements on it. Since he has the burden of all expenses he rarely uses commercial fertilizer, nor plants trees, nor allows the land to remain fallow for any extended period. The disadvantages are intensified in *métayage,* for the tenant may have to exchange most of the harvest simply to pay the owner. *Métayage* is profitable only on small, highly productive plots.

It is now almost impossible for a small cultivator to purchase enough land to become independent of tenancy. Note the sharp break, as shown in Table 2, between those with less than 1 hectare and those with more than 3.* A small amount of land simply cannot generate enough surplus to counter even the fragmentation caused by inheritance, let alone to permit acquisition of new lands. Each generation,

---

* I am grateful to Aram Yengoyan, of the University of Michigan, for this observation.

a number of those with 3 hectares and more will slide into the lower group; but almost no one climbs from it.

Productive Groups

The household provides most of the labor for the day-to-day operation of the farm. In the next chapters we shall examine the structure of the peasant household. We shall see who is numbered among its members, what are the stages of its development, and what is the relationship between a household and a family. Without responding to these questions here we may note that the adults perform most of the heavy labor preparing the fields, weeding them, harvesting the crops, and transporting them to the house or to the *bourg* for shipment to market. Young children help seed the fields and carry food and water to their parents. With their mothers they have the basic responsibility for the chickens and small animals; in the morning before going to school they gather vines for the rabbits and tie down the goats and sheep in fresher pasturage.

Men are paid between $1.75 and $2.25 a day, while women receive about $1.25. Wage laborers are supposed to be registered with social security, but only the largest employers who have regular needs for them list their workers and pay the required taxes. None of the *journaliers* in the village belongs to the union of agricultural workers, which has organized the sugarcane cutters.

The average cultivator regularly shares his labor with a handful of fellow villagers. These labor exchange groups are called *coups-de-main,* composed of three to six men who cooperate in the heavy work of land-clearing and harvesting. During the appropriate seasons they work on a regular schedule, each member having a turn in sequence. Usually they work as a group for the morning only, and return to their own fields in the afternoon. Each man brings his own tools and food. The person who is receiving the day provides rum and fruit juice, and if the work lasts for the entire day, the midday meal as well.

A *coup-de-main* may be composed of kinsmen, but the criteria for membership are similarity of age and control of comparable pieces of land. The latter criterion assures that a man will not have to give more labor than he receives. The criterion of age has to do with the egalitarian nature of exchange labor. A man who hosts the *coup-de-main* is the chief for that day; he decides how the work is to be done and directs it. The villagers feel that it is improper to give orders to a much older person. Thus, the *coup-de-main* is a functional equivalent of the extended family in productivity, without the costs of supporting large numbers of people during the nonproductive phases of the agricultural cycle.

Although the men of a *coup-de-main* are likely to be good friends and spend much time together, the groups do not have any formal activities beyond pooling labor. They are not named, they have no internal hierarchy, and are not in competition with other groups. In other parts of the Caribbean, labor exchange groups are more complex, with officers, meetings, emblems, and musicians (Métraux 1951:73–86). In Morne-Paysan the people recall the times when as many as fifty workers would prepare a field, swinging their hoes in time to a song leader and four or five drummers. At certain points all the workers would throw their hoes in the air and try to catch them before they touched the ground. Such *garoulé* as they were called had no fixed membership and were organized by large landowners who feasted the men at the end of the work, contributing food and drink and providing a place where they could dance and sing all night. At least since the Second World War there has been no *garoulé* in the village.

Labor-sharing pervades much of village life. Women market and baby-sit for each other. A childless or aged couple may be loaned a young person to help with the household work. Almost all house building is done by cooperative labor, with only the professional mason and carpenter being paid. The volunteers make the cement blocks or in a wattle-and-daub house do the entire construction. I was proudly told by several villagers that even work for the commune is done by *coup-de-main* when funds are lacking to hire laborers. The addition to the Town Hall was built on this basis. During our stay in Morne-Paysan only those men in sympathy with the mayor or under obligation to him volunteered for public work.

Markets

Tourists, debarking from one of the many cruise ships which ply the Caribbean during the winter months, invariably include the large urban vegetable markets on their "must-see" itinerary. Colorful, noisy, and crowded, the West Indian markets have the same fascination for visitors as do those in Mexico, West Africa and the Congo, Paris, and the Lower East Side of New York. These markets are important as well for the anthropologist. As Sidney Mintz has written of Haiti, "To follow the movement of marketers and stock through the system is an ideal way to begin to study the economy and to trace the distribution of economic and political power in the society" (1960:112).

Peasant production in Morne-Paysan, as we have seen, is partly geared to household consumption and partly to sale in domestic markets. Sacks and baskets filled with fruit or vegetables weighing either 50 or 100 kilograms each, are carried from the fields in the evening and deposited on the steps of the church in the center of the *bourg*. Most sacks are labelled with the name of the farmer's wife and with the name of the woman who will sell the food in the market. Two buses leave the *bourg* each morning loaded with produce and arrive at the market in Fort-de-France before 8 A.M. Along the road the buses pick up more passengers and produce, and on the big market day of Saturday several hundred sacks may be tied down on top and fifty or more persons crowded inside with chickens, rabbits, and an occasional pig. Passengers enter the bus from the front, and the early ones find seats directly behind the driver. The two rows of benches are connected across the center aisle by jump seats, and as these are quickly occupied, later arrivals must climb over them on their way to the rear. As they make their way to a seat, women stop to greet friends and relatives with a kiss, and men shake hands. Once the bus has left the village, new passengers enter from the rear door, and repeat the process of filling places closest to it, so that the last passengers must climb over them to squeeze into a remaining place in the center.

Some of the passengers are farmers' wives who are going to the city to sell their own produce. Since they are not professional market sellers (called *revendeuses*), they do not have a regular stall or clientele. They spread their wares on the ground either along the wall of the market or outside in the street. They have to pay all the expenses of the market including bus transportation and market taxes for themselves and the produce, and porters' fees on each sack and basket. They also lose a day's labor at home. But they keep all the receipts. Peasant women often decide to sell in the market if they feel they can get an exceptionally good price for their produce or if they have some reason to be in the city anyway.

Most of the sellers, especially on weekdays, are full-time specialists. These *revendeuses* or *marchandes* receive food on consignment which they sell on commission. The narrow streets around the market are jammed with buses waiting for an opening along the curb, tediously maneuvering back and forth until they can park. As each bus arrives in the early morning a group of porters (*dockeurs*) runs out to meet it. The driver's assistant, usually a teen-age boy, stands on top and passes the sacks on to the heads of the *dockeurs* while shouting out the name of the woman to whom it is consigned. The *dockeurs* carry their enormous loads at a run, in order to make as many trips as possible. Each time they enter the market they must pass through a turnstile and pay 50 or 100 francs, depending upon the item and the quantity. A guard gives them receipts, and they are reimbursed by the *marchandes* plus an additional 50 francs per sack.

The same turnstiles are used both for entering and leaving, and during the rush hours of the morning they become so jammed that traffic halts. A woman heavily laden with a sack on her head and a package on one arm tries to pass through the turnstile claiming that she is unable to reach her money but if the guard will let her through she will quickly return with 50 francs. The guard refuses, and emphasizes his refusal by throwing a lever which locks the turnstile. The woman argues and insults the guard, his parents, and all his descendants, but finally sets down the packages, and finds the money which she angrily slams down. Meanwhile a crowd has gathered on both sides, including a large and impatient porter whose earnings depend on the number of trips he can make. As the woman pays, the guard releases the brake, and both streams collide. It is amazing that no baskets or sacks are dropped.

The market women torment the guards and dispute vigorously any assessment above the minimum. The conclusion is known in advance, for the guard always wins, but not without much good humored abuse.

When produce is consigned to a *revendeuse* she must pay all the expenses except transportation. Her commission is formally 10 percent, but the country women cannot know the exact selling price, and assume the professionals are cheating somewhat. The relationship between them is delicate, however, and a *revendeuse* is not likely to jeopardize her sources of supply by grossly understating her profits. Similarly, within the market a regular clientele develops, and favored customers are given a better selection or a little extra. For casual customers, buying in the market is a complex game of bargaining and bluffing. The price depends upon the availability of similar produce in the market, its condition, and the time of day. Prices are highest in the morning, as the produce arrives fresh. In the afternoon the price drops considerably but the food is much handled and less attractive. Unsold food is stored beneath the tables in the locked market. Of course peasant women who come in to sell do not have storage facilities and must either dispose of their unsold merchandise for very low prices or return with it to the villages.

Fruits and vegetables are not the only items sold in the "great market" (so called in distinction to the smaller markets for fish and butchered meat). Many women also deal in small live animals, like chickens and rabbits, and eggs. Some are specialists in spices, and others sell only imported, manufactured items, such as religious books, pictures, and medals, or colognes, hair oils and combs. A few stock medicinal plants. One section of the market is devoted to florists. Another section features work from the two main handicraft regions of the island: carafes, vases, and flowerpots from the potteries around Trois Islets, on the old estate of Empress Josephine Tascher de la Pagerie; and intricate and highly distinctive basketry from the Morne-des-Esses *quartier* above Ste. Marie. (This basketry, an apparent survival of Carib techniques in weaving and dyeing, is produced today only in Martinique, Dominica, and British Guiana.) Across the street from the market are hardware and drygoods shops, which appeal particularly to rural folk, and a wholesale buyer of cacao. There are also many small bars.

Several hundred women sell in the market at one time, and there are inevitable variations in price among them. Many customers are market experts also, and are as quick to perceive a seller's willingness to drop the price as the latter is to sense the buyer's readiness to go a little higher. Almost nothing is offered immediately at the "last price." The customer has an edge if she has the exact change. She states the price she is willing to pay and while bargaining stuffs her basket. The *revendeuse* must then accept the price or unpack the basket. If change has to be made the advantage shifts, for the seller can stall and argue while holding her customer's money.

Revendeuses keep the same location in the market for years, where they are easily found by their customers. Those in proximity form cooperative relationships. They watch each others' stalls, make change, and even sell for each other. If a regular client shows up and her seller is not there, neighboring sellers do not try to entice her but ask her to wait until her steady seller returns.

Not all the selling goes on in the large market. Many women wander the streets of the city, hawking foods from baskets on their heads. Others set up little stalls near the bus depots or along the docks. Some women come to market every morning very early and buy food for resale outside the city. Because they are the most regular and largest customers, they pay a little less and charge their customers more. They may, in turn, provision a number of other sellers, especially young girls just beginning a career. Thus, although it is possible for the peasant, or his wife, to sell directly to the consumer, there is commonly at least one and sometimes several intermediaries between producer and consumer. In such cases, the amount of produce handled by the last seller is very, very small. She moves up the scale as she is

Market women examining bananas and coconuts. The woman on the left wears the long dress, waist kerchief, and headdress now characteristic of older women. The younger woman on the right wears a shorter dress.

able to invest larger sums, until she can afford the investment, and risks, of operating in the market itself. In addition to the markets in Fort-de-France, each large town has a market place. A few women in Morne-Paysan prefer to make the shorter trip to St. Pierre, where the pace is much slower and the atmosphere calmer.

After unloading at the market, the bus drivers spend the rest of the day in the city purchasing items for people in the village. They buy grocery supplies wholesale for a rural shop, sacks of cement for a mason, galvanized iron roofing, and the like, and finally park at a terminal not far from the market. In the early afternoon they begin the two-hour trip back. Following the coastal road, the buses pass through a fishing village just before climbing the final hill to Morne-Paysan. The open *gommiers* or fishing canoes are drawn up on the beach, and the fishermen are hanging their nets to dry on great bamboo poles. The *gommiers* are small wooden boats, typically with crews of two or three men, occasionally with a few more. Outboard motors are becoming common, supplementing the oars and small square sails that have propelled the canoes at least since the days of Père Labat. Like the buses, the boats are painted in gay bright colors. Religious names are most common, such as *Volonté de Dieu, St. Antoine, Filius Die, Ste.-Croix de Jésus, Grace au Seigneur, L'Immaculé Conception, Dieu Merci, Regina Coeli, Reine des Anges, Confiance en Dieu,* and *Bonté de Ste. Thérèse*. Many names are aphorisms, in French and Creole, like "*J'ai tort d'avoir raison,*" "*Revenue de mes enfants,*" "*Faites comme moi,*" "*La parole est libre,*" "*L'union fait la force*" (perhaps a survival from the war-time days of Vichy rule), "*fe sa zot le*" ("do what they want"), and "*di sa zot le*" ("say what they want"). Others are named after people or natural objects, particularly marine objects, like *L'Océan, L'Etoile de Nuit, Grain de Sable.*

Fishermen use traps and nets. Formerly of bamboo, most traps are now made of chicken wire. They are set at the bottom of the sea, usually no more than a quarter-mile from the shore. About once a week they are visited, and emptied of whatever lobster or other crustacea may have entered. Coastal net-fishing requires a team of two boats, with as many as six men in each. The net is spread between the boats with lines extending to the shore. As many as fifty people may help pull the lines to draw the nets in, as the men in the boats beat the water to keep the fish from swimming out of the nets. The nets may be emptied and reset as often as four times a day. Since they are placed close to shore, the catch is mostly of small fish, like mackerel, *coubirou* and *totoblo.* More remunerative, though riskier, is fishing at the coastal limits (the *miquelon*), in which two men in a single boat try to net the larger prizes of red snapper, tuna, shark and swordfish. The important runs of these fish are in September, which is also the center of the hurricane season, and the seas are usually heavy and often hazardous. Fishermen divide the sales among the crew, and the owners of the boat, motor, and net.

Persons returning to Morne-Paysan buy fish through the windows of the bus, and place them in metal or open calabash bowls brought for that purpose. Fishermen do not deal directly with consumers, but sell to women mongers who resell to travelers along the road which passes within 10 yards of the boats. A few women buy fish for resale in the country. One woman in Morne-Paysan walks 5 to 8 kilometers each way buying fish on the coast for resale in the village. Fish do not keep, of course, and the *vendeuse* buys only as much as she can reasonably dispose of in one day. Her total equipment is a basket and a scale. There is a regular market in Fort-de-France and a section of the market in St. Pierre devoted to fish, where the more active entrepreneurs operate, dealing with more urban clienteles.

The buses announce their return from the city with a long honking. People gather around to greet the travelers and to find out how the market went. Often among the passengers is someone who has been absent from the village for a while, away at school or in the army, and the people greet him warmly. Men and boys help the driver's assistant unload the cargo. Newspapers arrive by bus, and men will retire to bars to discuss the reported events and to rest before returning to work.

True higglers, women who travel around the country buying and reselling, are rare today in Martinique. The remarkable Lafcadio Hearn, who spent several years in Martinique during the 1880s, was much taken by these *porteuses,* who were walking commissaries dealing in local and imported produce. If we are to believe Hearn (1890:105), these women were capable of carrying a burden of one hundred and twenty to one hundred and fifty pounds weight and of walking fifty miles a day. Their baskets were so heavy that they needed help in placing and removing them from their heads. In Hearn's day, "no one but a brute will ever refuse to aid a woman to lift or to relieve herself of her burden;—you may see the wealthiest merchant, the proudest planter, gladly do it;—the meanness of refusing, or of making any conditions for the performance of this little kindness has only been imagined in those strange Stories of Devils wherewith the oral and uncollected literature of the creole abounds" (Hearn:105–106).

Although the total handle of goods and money passing through the local markets is considerable—as reflected in the revenues collected by the municipality from the tax on buses, goods entering the market, and stalls—this handle is the sum of an enormous number of small exchanges. There are persons in the government and elsewhere who hope to "rationalize" the sale of vegetables by organizing producers cooperatives or otherwise encouraging wholesale distribution. They feel that the current market system is atavistic, with its thousands of small retailers and the many intermediary steps between the producer and the consumer. The inevitable price increase at each step, they argue, does not aid the producer.

What does exist in the internal distribution of locally raised produce is an integration of scale. Small cultivators regularly harvest a sack or two of produce beyond the demands of domestic consumption, and consign it to a *revendeuse* who may sell for about a dozen farmers. The bus owner is a small businessman, who transports the merchandise frequently albeit with a far greater investment than the farmer or market merchant. Finally, it is sold in small amounts to consumers, who shop daily or at least several times a week. Whatever its disadvantages may be, the system has certain clear advantages. The major one is that it can be entered at any level (except perhaps that of transporter) with a small investment. The farmer who intercrops a small field in order to reduce his vulnerability to failure, enters the market regularly thereby insuring a regular if small income throughout the harvest. The *revendeuse* can afford to buy or accept on consignment quantities which the farmers send her, without elaborate warehouse facilities, and without overwhelming problems of bookkeeping. The consumer can exploit the existence of a plurality of suppliers insisting on a good price. She can also be guaranteed reasonably fresh produce since small storage facilities preclude keeping vegetables more than a day or so. And the thousands of women who deal in produce, many from households in which there is no employed male, are absorbed into the economy.

Throughout this brief description of marketing the central role of women has been emphasized. The peasant's wife supervises the movement of goods to the city and may accompany it to the market. If she does not market herself, she makes the arrangements with a *revendeuse* or with a friend or relative to sell for her. She is responsible for keeping accounts and handling the receipts of sales. Although men sell in the meat market, all vegetables and fruit are sold by women. And women do almost all buying in the market.

Some have suggested that the almost exclusive female domination of the market is a survival of West African marketing in which women also are prominent. Whatever the historical explanation for it, the economic role of women in Martinique has profound implications for the structure of the peasant household. In the next chapter we shall examine this household in detail.

5

The Household

WE HAVE FOUND it necessary in Martinique to distinguish the family, which is based upon kinship, from the domestic group or household, based on coresidence and food-sharing. A "household" includes those persons who habitually reside in the same structure and who have a common fund for consumptive use. Corporate productivity, particularly in farming and marketing, is a frequent but not necessary condition for the unit. Households and families differ, of course, even in societies in which there is an unequivocal emphasis on the nuclear or conjugal family—that is, a pair of mating adults and their offspring—for the domestic group may contain fewer or more members. The normal sequence of family development among the middle class in the United States, for example, contains three main types: (1) the household of a young, childless couple; (2) the household of a couple and their children; (3) the household of the older couple whose children have left to form households of their own. There are also households of single persons; of divorced or widowed adults and children; of parents, children, and grandchildren; of couples, siblings and children; and so forth. The typical domestic cycle is derived from the separation of generations upon marriage, because conjugality is emphasized over descent, and from the expectation that marriage at least precede procreation, if not also mating.

The empirical material for this chapter is a sample of 94 households, about a third of all domestic units in Morne-Paysan. They contain 494 persons. The presentation and analysis of the data rely heavily on the important comparative study of West Indian family structures by Michael G. Smith (1962).

In Martinique, and in some other parts of the West Indies, consensual sexual cohabitation within a household frequently follows a period of extraresidential mating, in which the partners live in separate homes, and is often deferred until the woman is pregnant. Consensual cohabitation almost always precedes marriage, the public ceremonialization of mating, which is delayed usually until some and often all children have been born. Thus late adolescents and young adults tend to mate extraresidentially; middle-aged adults are more likely to cohabit consensually, and marriage is elected by older persons. The sequence is demonstrated in the following tables.

TABLE 3

MARITAL STATUS OF ADULT MALES CLASSIFIED BY AGE

	15–24		25–39		40–54		55–69		70+	
	No.	%	No.	%	No.	%	No.	%	No.	%
Single, childless	26	92.9	5	16.7	3	10.7	1	7.1	0	0.0
Single, parent	0	0.0	2	6.7	0	0.0	0	0.0	0	0.0
Consensually cohabiting	2	7.1	13	43.3	3	10.7	0	0.0	0	0.0
Married	0	0.0	10	33.3	22	78.6	10	71.5	3	75.0
Widowed	0	0.0	0	0.0	0	0.0	3	21.4	1	25.0
TOTALS	28	100.0	30	100.0	28	100.0	14	100.0	4	100.0

TABLE 4

MARITAL STATUS OF ADULT FEMALES CLASSIFIED BY AGE

	15–24		25–39		40–54		55–69		70+	
	No.	%	No.	%	No.	%	No.	%	No.	%
Single, childless	24	68.6	3	7.9	4	12.1	3	27.3	3	30.0
Single, parent	4	11.4	5	13.2	3	9.1	1	9.1	0	0.0
Consensually cohabiting	5	14.3	12	31.6	3	9.1	0	0.0	0	0.0
Married	2	5.7	17	44.7	17	51.5	5	45.5	1	10.0
Widowed	0	0.0	1	2.6	6	18.2	2	18.1	6	60.0
TOTALS	35	100.0	38	100.0	33	100.0	11	100.0	10	100.0

These figures alone do not negate the possibility of culture change. Interviews with married persons, however, reveal a prior history of consensual coresidence, and, in turn, persons in the latter relationship claim an earlier pattern of extraresidential mating. These conjugal patterns are examined in detail in the following chapter. In this chapter we shall discuss the kinds of household structures which are found in the village, and attempt to explain their significance.

The Sample

Table 5 shows the distribution of the sample population by sex and age. While there is almost exact overall sexual parity—248 women and 246 men—women outnumber men by 1.2 to 1 in the reproductive age-group 15 through 54. This group accounts for only 39 percent of the population; some 53 percent are

TABLE 5

POPULATION OF THE SAMPLE HOUSEHOLDS, CLASSIFIED BY SEX AND AGE

	Number			*Percentage*			Females per Male
Age	Male	Female	Total	Male	Female	Total	
0–4	49	45	94	9.92	9.11	19.03	.92
5–14	93	76	169	18.83	15.38	34.21	.82
15–24	28	35	63	5.67	7.09	12.75	1.25
25–39	30	38	68	6.07	7.69	13.76	1.27
40–54	28	33	61	5.67	6.68	12.35	1.18
55–69	14	11	25	2.83	2.23	5.06	.79
70 and over	4	10	14	0.81	2.02	2.83	2.50
TOTAL	246	248	494	49.8	50.2	100.0	1.01

below 15 years of age, and the rest, 8 percent, are 55 years and older. This distribution of ages implies rather high death rates among older persons, and, since death rates for infants were high until the completion of the maternity hospital in 1951, high birth rates as well.

Tables 6 and 7 show the distribution of household headship. We determined who was head by asking members of the household and by verifying the response with nonmembers. Outsiders named the head by saying "That is the house of so-and-so. . ." In every case the judgments corresponded. Two-thirds of domestic units are headed by men, and acquisition of headship is achieved by three-fourths of the men age 25 years and older. One-third of the households are headed by women and only about 40 percent of the women ever achieve headship. As we shall see, female headship is not primarily a function of widowhood, but of women heading homes in which there is no conjugal cohabitation. At any one time, 59 percent of the adult men head households, against only 26 percent of adult women.

Table 8 shows the range of household sizes, from units containing one to eighteen persons. The mean size is 5.26. If we exclude those households with only one member, the mean size is 5.82. There is a tendency for households headed by

TABLE 6

HEADS OF THE SAMPLE HOUSEHOLDS, CLASSIFIED BY SEX AND AGE

	Number			*Percentage*		
Age	Male	Female	Total	Male	Female	Total
15–24	2	2	4	2.13	2.13	4.26
25–39	22	9	31	23.40	9.57	32.97
40–54	21	14	35	22.34	14.89	37.23
55–69	13	4	17	13.82	4.26	18.08
70 and over	3	4	7	3.19	4.26	7.45
TOTAL	61	33	94	64.9	35.1	100.0

TABLE 7

DISTRIBUTION OF HOUSEHOLD HEADSHIP AMONG ADULT MEMBERS OF THE SAMPLE POPULATION CLASSIFIED BY SEX AND AGE

	Male			*Female*			*Both Sexes*
Age	Total	Male HHs	% HHs	Total	Female HHs	% HHs	% HHs
15–24	28	2	7.1	35	2	5.7	6.4
25–39	30	22	73.3	38	9	23.7	45.6
40–54	28	21	75.0	33	14	42.4	57.4
55–69	14	13	92.9	11	4	36.4	68.0
70 and over	4	3	75.0	10	4	40.0	50.0
TOTAL	104	61	58.7	127	33	26.0	40.7

men to be larger than those headed by women, although women head the two largest households in the sample.

TABLE 8

HOUSEHOLDS OF THE SAMPLE, CLASSIFIED BY SEX OF HEAD AND NUMBER OF PERSONS

	Sex of Head			*Total Persons*		
Number of Persons	Male	Female	Total	Male*	Female*	Total
1	6	5	11	6	5	11
2	5	5	10	10	10	20
3	5	5	10	15	15	30
4	8	4	12	32	16	48
5	5	4	9	25	20	45
6	8	4	12	48	24	72
7	12	1	13	84	7	91
8	1	2	3	8	16	24
9	3	1	4	27	9	36
10	5	0	5	50	0	50
11	2	0	2	22	0	22
12	1	0	1	12	0	12
15	0	1	1	0	15	15
18	0	1	1	0	18	18
TOTAL	61	33	94	339	155	494
Excluding persons living alone	55	28	83	333	150	483
Averages: including solitary persons				5.56	4.70	5.26 persons per house
excluding solitary persons				6.05	5.36	5.82 persons per house

* Household heads.

Varieties of Domestic Units

Three principal types of households are found in the village: households of single persons; households headed by a single adult; and households which contain a conjugal pair.

Although only 2 percent of the people in the sample live by themselves, they constitute almost 12 percent of the households.

TABLE 9

HOUSEHOLDERS LIVING ALONE, CLASSIFIED BY AGE, SEX, AND MARITAL STATUS

	Male						Female					
	−24	−39	−54	−69	70+	Total	−24	−39	−54	−69	70+	Total
Never married	0	1	0	1	0	2	1	1	2	0	0	4
Married, separated	0	0	0	1	1	2	0	0	0	0	0	0
Married, widowed	0	0	0	2	0	2	0	0	0	1	0	1
TOTAL	0	1	0	4	1	6	1	1	2	1	0	5

Five of the six men who live alone are 55 years or older. Only one of the five women who live alone is in that age group. Since there are eighteen men and twenty-one women in the sample ages 55 and over, men are more than five times as likely to end their careers in solitary living than are women. All of the men who were married and one of the bachelors have children, but the father-child tie is often tenuous and may not provide the basis for a durable relationship. This is demonstrated by the prominence of women heads in households which have only one percent present:

TABLE 10

HOUSEHOLD HEADS WITHOUT RESIDENT MATES

Composition of Household	Male Head	Female Head
Head plus children	2	16
Head plus grandchildren	0	1
Head plus children and grandchildren	1	2
TOTAL	3	19

The composition of households headed by women differs markedly from those headed by men. As expected they differ in the presence of mates, since only five households headed by women include a resident mate, whereas fifty-two households headed by men include a mate. This affects also the number of household members who are descended from the mate but not from the head. The principal difference in composition of the domestic unit, however, is the striking frequency of collateral kin, particularly siblings and their descendants, in units with female heads, and their almost total absence in units with male heads.

TABLE 11

COMPOSITION OF HOUSEHOLDS CLASSIFIED BY RELATIONSHIP TO HEAD

	Male Head		*Female Head*	
Relationship to Head	No.	Percent	No.	Percent
Mates	52	18.7	5	4.1
Descendants	194	69.8	81	66.4
Mates' descendants by others	21	7.6	0	0.0
Siblings and descendants	2	0.7	23*	18.9
Parents	0	0.0	2	1.6
Other (collaterals of parents, sibling's mate, adopted children)	9	3.2	11	9.0
TOTAL	278	100.0	122	100.0

* 18 of these are sisters' descendants.

Although the percentage of descendants in male- and female-headed households is very close—69.8 and 66.4 respectively—94 percent are actual children of a male head, against only 80 percent for female heads. Domestic units headed by women, therefore, are more than three times as likely to include grandchildren and great-grandchildren. Since male-headed households usually include a resident mate, and the couple is often married or planning to marry, the frequency of legitimate and recognized children is also much higher than in female-headed households. This can be seen in the following Table.

TABLE 12

BIRTH STATUS OF RESIDENT CHILDREN

	Male Head		*Female Head*	
Birth Status	No.	Percent	No.	Percent
Legitimate	138	75.0	28	43.0
Recognized	29	16.0	7	11.0
Natural	16	9.0	30	46.0
TOTAL	183	100.0	65	100.0

Nine children, all male, live with their fathers. In five cases the father is widowed, and in two he is separated from the mother. Two children live with their fathers and fathers' wife. Seventy-nine children—25 boys and 54 girls—live with their mothers apart from their fathers. Forty of these—1 boy and 39 girls—live alone with their mothers. Twenty-six—13 boys and 13 girls—are in homes in which their mother is consensually cohabiting, and 6, all boys, live with their mothers and mothers' husbands. The other 7 children—5 boys and 2 girls—live in homes which include mothers' grandparents, and mothers' grandparents' siblings.

Twenty-eight children reside with neither parent. Eighteen of these live with mothers' kinsmen, four with fathers' kinsmen, and six with nonkin. As M. G. Smith writes (1962:80) of the peasant village Latante on Grenada:

> Given three alternative mating forms, each with its own definition of parental roles, a multiplicity of alternatives for the domestic placement of children is well-nigh unavoidable. The multiplicity of mating forms itself rules out the possibility that all the children not living with both their parents will be found within one alternative type of domestic group.

Fifty-seven households—61 percent of the sample—include a conjugal or sexually cohabiting pair; no household includes more than one. Thus while many units count members of three or more generations, they are not structurally "extended" or "joint" families, for they do not contain a nuclear family of orientation *and* a nuclear family of procreation.

TABLE 13

HOUSEHOLDS BASED ON CONJUGALITY

	Male Head		*Female Head*	
Type	Consensual Coresidence	Marriage	Consensual Coresidence	Marriage
Couple without children	2	5	0	0
Couple and children	13	25	4	1
Couple, children, and grandchildren	0	4	0	0
Couple and grandchildren	0	3	0	0
TOTAL	15	37	4	1

Women in a conjugal relationship rarely head households, and only one married woman is a household head; she is a remarried widow who owns her house and piece of land. Most men, on the other hand, in households with resident mates are married, and the seven households which include persons of three generations are all headed by married men.

A Case Study of Household Variation

Henri Navarre, born a slave, was emancipated in 1848, left the coastal plantation where he had labored, and become a tenant farmer in the hills above Morne-Paysan. Cultivation was profitable and he was able to purchase 2 hectares contiguous to the land he farmed. He married the daughter of a man freed many years before and had twelve children, all born legitimate. Four sons purchased land also, the largest lot being almost 6 hectares. In total the family owned and worked cooperatively about twenty hectares, and they were considered economically well-off among the freed population. Four of Henri's daughters died childless spinsters, one is a spinster at 97, and one son never married. Six children married, and most of their descendants continue to live in the original *quartier*.

Navarre's oldest son had nine children. When he died in 1944 the land, according to the records of the surveyor, was "subject to a friendly division in nine equal lots" of 0.65 hectare. In addition, the heirs received 1/108th each of the original holding. One of these heirs died and left a childless widow, but the others are living and all but one girl who married out of the village are on the property.

A glance at the Navarre family chart reveals a large number of alternative household compositions. Most common are households containing a nuclear family, often with additional children of the woman. These nuclear households are better adapted than larger groupings to the small size of the holdings, and the egalitarian nature of kinship relations within a generation does not encourage the differential distribution of authority associated with the extended household. Labor-exchange groups, as we discussed in Chapter 4, are functional alternatives to large families when labor demands are greatest, such as during field-clearing, planting, and harvesting. Household No. 14, containing a woman and her children, her sister, sister's mate, their children, and sister's children from a previous *ménage,* approaches joint domesticity; however, it was in process of dissolution during the field study, and each mother had her own kitchen hut, one on either side of the two-room *case*.

While most of the households are nuclear, joint and extended household settlements are found, the result of the fractionalization of holdings and the construction of a new house on family land when a boy starts a *ménage*. The *quartier,* in the last two generations, then, has become largely a kin settlement and exogamous, because most persons are too closely related to marry. Even in these cases, however, where the amount of land associated with each household is too small for profitable exploitation, we rarely find reconsolidation into larger, compound-exploited plots. The limits of each person's holding are well defined and cultivation is generally restricted to the owner or to his tenants.

While redivision, therefore, has resulted in a number of related households in close proximity, the system of closed fields, introduced into Martinique by Breton and Norman settlers, continues in force. Since a person inherits from both parents it is likely that he will own lands separated from each other, often at considerable distance. The group of siblings, however, do not agree to set aside one inheritance for homesites and maintain the undivided integrity of the larger holding for cultivation. Cooperation is more likely to mean reciprocal baby-sitting and marketing, with one of the wives marketing the produce of several siblings.

Household No. 1 is composed of Mlle. Nicole Navarre, a sister, and her father's sister. While not a typical household, this kind does occur among elderly spinsters who have never entered nonlegal unions. It seems to be related to a combination of ultimogeniture, that is, inheritance by the youngest child, and relatively high status, either through education, possession of large pieces of land, or light

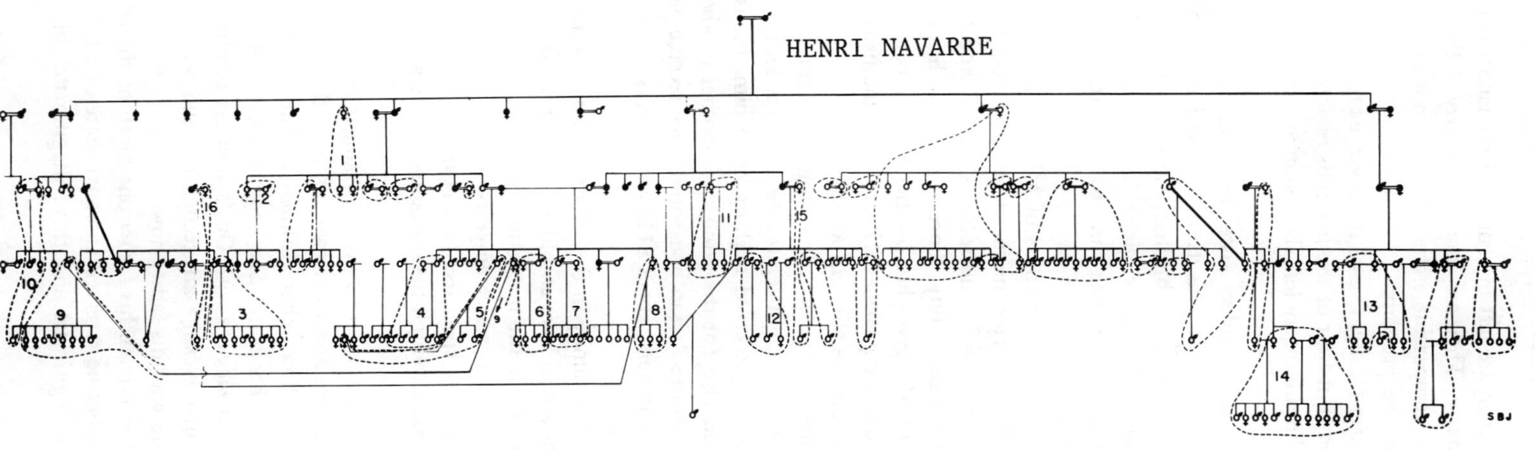
THE DESCENDANTS of HENRI NAVARRE
HENRI NAVARRE
1
2
3
4
5
6
7
8
9
10
11
12
13
14
15
16
SBJ
Marriage
Deceased
Consensual Coresidence
7
Household (Nos. refer to text)

skin color. Such women are left in control of the land when their brothers move out and their sisters marry. They are unable to marry within the village because they cannot find men of comparable status. They do not marry out in order not to lose effective control of the property.

In the Navarre family, five of the seven daughters of the founder never married or had children. But four of the five sons established families in Morne-Paysan. One of the girls who did marry left the commune and the management of her property to the others.

Nicole and her coresident sister have combined their holdings which total 1.3 hectares about the house plus lands received from their paternal grandfather and from his siblings who died childless. Since they have no descendants, their land will pass to the families of their siblings. They prefer to hire workers, often nephews, to cultivate the land, rather than to lease it. Marketing is consigned to a professional (*revendeuse*).

Household No. 2 is composed of Michelle Navarre and her husband. They had five children, all born after the marriage. One died, two are married and live in the village, and two have left. She sold a piece of land to her daughter (No. 3), and a portion to the municipality. Since her brother has taken in her husband as a *colon* (sharecropper), she gives her brother full rights of cultivation on her part of the inheritance in another *quartier*. This is quite the usual situation; work is often provided for the conjugal relatives of kinsmen.

As in the case above, Michelle's daughter, Jeanne (No. 3) obtained the land from her mother. She has eight legitimate children. Her husband was never recognized by his father and received nothing from him. He is a *colon* for his wife's mother's brother and also for the widow of another brother of his mother-in-law. As is true of many Morne-Paysan households they receive part of their income from family assistance; the amount, about $115 annually, is determined by the number and ages of their children.

This is the only family in the village in which a man supervises the marketing. It is very important to have an older daughter to take care of the children while the mother works or to do the marketing. Jeanne's oldest daughter is in school, and so marketing is done by her sixteen-year-old son. He does not sell directly to the consumer but to a market specialist (*marchande*). (No men sell directly in any of the vegetable markets, although they do some of the selling of fish and most of the meat.)

Guy Navarre is a son of Nicole's younger brother Félix. He lives (No. 4) with his mistress Juliette and their two children, the older of whom is recognized. In addition there are three other children of Juliette, two boys from her second *ménage* and one from her third. She has had eleven children with four men. One of her daughters is *en ménage* with Guy's younger brother (No. 5). Juliette's four children from her first *ménage* are recognized and will inherit from their father. One of them is living with his father now.

Guy will receive from his father one-ninth of the latter's 0.65-hectare inheritance. From his mother he received an equal share of a holding of 0.5-hectare to be divided among nine legitimate and three illegitimate children. Guy and four siblings have built homes on that inheritance. Juliette plants a kitchen garden and occasionally finds a day's work in the sugar fields. She gets some money from a son in the city. Guy is a tenant for a nonrelative and sometimes works for his father's sister Nicole.

Guy's brother (No. 5) has built his home on the inheritance from his mother. His mistress is the daughter of Guy's mistress. They have two children, both unrecognized. The couple claims to have no interest in marriage. They have been living consensually for three years, since she was seventeen. Apart from a kitchen garden which she cultivates they rent no land, both finding occasional wage employment.

Hubert (No. 6) is the only married child of Félix Navarre, having wed in 1950 when his wife was fifteen. They have four children, the oldest a girl born three months after the marriage, who lives with her mother's widowed mother. The others live with their parents. As have Christian and Guy, Hubert built on his mother's land. He sharecrops land of one of the large proprietors in Morne-Paysan, and his wife markets. He is one of the few small planters who has taken the chance of putting the greatest part of the land he rents into a cash crop, bananas. He also owns some cattle.

Roger (No. 7), Josephine (No. 8), and Elizabeth are illegitimate children of the wife of Félix Navarre. Roger and Josephine have homes in close proximity to those of Guy, Christian, and Hubert. Josephine, who was never recognized, lives with her three children fathered by the husband of Jeanne Navarre (No. 3). There is no marketing because her garden gives no surplus, and she works as a day-laborer for about $1.25 on a nearby farm. Roger and Elizabeth were recognized by their father and received from him an hectare of land. They both married, Roger to a woman from another village, with whom he has four surviving children, three born after the marriage. Although Elizabeth's five children have title to half the inheritance of her father, Roger works the entire hectare, since Elizabeth died and her children live with their father in another *quartier* where he has land. Roger also rents land and animals in *colonage*. His wife does the marketing.

For seven years Josephine shared her house with her half-sister Robertine, Robertine's lover Scholastique, and their children. The couple now lives on the land of Scholastique's father's mother (No. 9). This family demonstrates that lack of formal marriage does not necessarily imply an instable household, for they have been together fourteen years and have nine children, of whom six are recognized. They claim to be saving for a marriage. Eight of the children live with them, and one son lives with his father's parents (No. 10). The couple has not only a conjugal relationship, but also share descent, for Robertine is Scholastique's second cousin.

Kin-mating is not uncommon in the village. One large family was founded in the 1890's by the marriage of a man to his father's brother's daughter. They were natural children of brothers, and since the fathers were legally unknown, no religious dispensation was needed for the marriage. The fathers, white, transferred large amounts of land to the couple by sale in which no money actually changed hands, and the family today is one of the largest landowners in Morne-Paysan.

The structure of households Nos. 11, 12, and 13 parallels that of No. 4.

Each is composed of a *ménage* couple, their children, and children of the woman from at least two earlier *ménages*. No. 13 is interesting in that it is onc of the extremely rare instances of a married man having abandoned his wife to establish a household with another woman. Adulterous coresidence is most strongly condemned by the Church, and the couple has been denied access to the sacraments.

The inheritance in Household No. 13 is rather complex. Her father left .25 hectare among seven children. In addition she received one-eightyfourth of the original holding of Henri Navarre. Her brother died leaving no children legally able to succeed, and his property was divided among the surviving siblings, leaving her 3.6 hectares. She claims that her father never accepted the division of Henri Navarre's holding, and she is considering trying to force a legal redistribution. She and two siblings have built homes on the 0.25 hectare left by their father.

6

The Round of Life: Marriage and Other Matings

THE SOCIAL STRUCTURE of the village—of any village, band, or tribe—has to do with the particular location of individuals and the ways in which they behave and are expected to behave toward each other and outsiders. Sex and age are two invariable criteria of placement in human societies. The difference between these reference points of status ascription is, of course, the stability of the one and fluidity of the other. Anthropologists have become interested in the movement of individuals through the social structure, in how persons are recruited and trained to fill specific social positions at particular times, and how these age-associated status changes are ritualized and made public. Robert Redfield has pointed out that each culture has a "characteristic human career" or a "typical biography." Just as each culture deals uniquely with nature's periodic cycles, so it does with human organic development. While every society must account for the physical maturation of its members, no two impose precisely the same rhythm of social maturation. The cultural recognition and ceremonialization of birth, puberty, mating, illness, aging, and death are called rites of passage by anthropologists, and we have come to expect that these events are ritualized in all cultures. Because of this expectation, the discovery that the ritualization of mating—that is, marriage—is frequently omitted as a station in the typical Caribbean career and, when it does occur, has no fixed sequential relationship to childbearing, has invoked much theoretical discussion and controversy.

If a casual visitor were to ask a rural Martiniquan how people ought to marry, he would be told that the ceremony must be preceded by a period of courtship, during which the couple is always chaperoned by a female relative or godparent of the girl. The suitor makes his intentions known to her parents by asking someone respected by both families to advance his claims and present him in a favorable light. Following the civil rites in the town hall required by French law, a wedding is held in the church. The bride wears the long white veil to which she is entitled as a virgin (*jeune fille*). After the ceremony there is a procession from the church to a house in the village for a reception (*fête*), with food, drink, and dancing to an orchestra. At midnight the newlyweds slip out to begin the honeymoon, which inaugurates life-long monogamous coresidence and childbearing.

In fact, this *jeune fille* marriage almost never occurs in the village. Most coresidential unions are based merely on consent, rather than on formal marriage. Most marriage rites follow a period of consensual coresidence during which children are conceived and often born. In order to encourage marriage the priests waived the expectation of virginity for wearing the long veil, but the villagers insist upon it themselves. A girl who married a month before the birth of her first child said she could not wear the veil because of public ridicule, even though the priest permitted it. At another ceremony the bride did wear the veil to the stage-whispered amusement of the people milling about outside the church, since she was visibly pregnant.

Marriages which follow a period of coresidence, and which may occur after the birth of children or even after menopause are called *béni commerce* or *béni peché.* A church ceremony is held; but there is no veil, no procession through the streets, and no honeymoon.

Other than the couple and their witnesses, very few people attend a *béni commerce.* The reception is still held, and one young couple who had lived *en ménage* for several years and had two children were married at 5 A.M. in order, they said, not to have a *fête.* The bride quietly returned home to her children, and the groom took his hoe and left for the fields. Many persons living *en ménage* claim that their inability to afford a *fête* is their main obstacle to marriage, and the church, in consequence, has tried to convince them to marry without it. Some people hope to save enough money to have the *fête,* but money is hard to accumulate, and other needs too often impose.

At a typical *fête* all the people of the *quartier* and the friends and relatives of the couple come. No one, even if uninvited, is turned away. Each person is welcomed by the bride and groom who sit in rocking chairs at one end of the room. An orchestra of four teen-age brothers plays continuously from about five in the afternoon until two in the morning. The leader plays the melodies on a concertina. The other boys are the rhythm section: one has a bass drum hit with a foot pedal, a sort of snare drum, and a wood block and cymbal; the second thumps a warped guitar, with a missing top string and a dead bass string. The guitar is never chorded. The youngest boy plays maracas. The musicians sit in the center of one wall in the long narrow room, and dancers keep bumping into the bass drum. The couple lead the first dance, a waltz. People prefer traditional Martiniquan dances, like the mazourka and biguine, which the orchestra plays for the rest of the evening. A few people complain that they are no longer danced in the classic manner. (A folklore group has been organized in the city to reteach traditional Martiniquan music and dance.) Most adults, even the elderly, dance without remaining with the same partner. There is no cutting in, however, except when men separate girls dancing together.

Children run around freely, eating cakes and drinking sodas. Each time the bride and groom get up to dance, some children sit in the rocking chairs, relinquishing them when the couple returns. The children stay until the end of the festivities, although some fall asleep on the floor. Adults also eat cakes and drink wine and rum. Around midnight the bride throws her veil and gloves to the unmarried girls, and the couple slips out of the party. The girl who catches the veil is to be the next to marry.

Consensual coresidence without marriage in Martinique is called living *en ménage,* and corresponds to what is termed "living with" or "faithful concubinage" in the English-speaking West Indies. The majority of villagers live *en ménage* at some time during their lives, and almost all marriages are preceded by a period of consensual coresidence. Some *ménages* endure for the entire adult lives of the couple, but many persons in the community have had several such relationships. A first *ménage,* especially of a young girl, typically follows a period of extraresidential mating, during which the girl has become pregnant. A girl may not receive a lover at home if she lives with her parents, but the fields and woods provide ample facilities for trysting. If the girl is living with both parents, her lover must request permission from her father to establish the household. Permission is usually granted if the girl is pregnant, because consensual cohabitation is preferred to an unmarried mother's living with her parents. The fact that the young man is willing to assume the responsibility of a household, even if unwilling to marry, is taken as a sign of good intentions. The girl's parents may hope that the relationship will someday be regularized in marriage, as it may well be. If the young man does not take the initiative, the girl's father may encourage him by offering financial assistance or, more commonly, land on which to build a house.

The division of labor for *ménage* couples is the same as that for married ones. The man works in the fields and with the larger animals. The woman takes care of the children, supervises the marketing of farm produce, and works in the kitchen garden and with the small animals. She usually controls family finances, giving the man an allowance from market sale of vegetables. She has jurisdiction over family allocations from the government and over any income derived from her garden, or from working as a laundress or seamstress. It is her obligation to see that the family is properly fed and clothed. When the household is established, the man (or his family) is expected to furnish the kitchen-dining room (dishes, table, chairs), and the woman furnishes the bedroom (bed, mattress, bureau).

Since marriage usually follows a period of consensual cohabitation, a woman's first children are likely to be born illegitimate. During the civil rites at the town hall, the couple announce the names and ages of the children to be legitimized, some of whom may themselves already be parents. During three years for which we have information (1928, 1931, 1936) there were twenty-three marriages in the village. Twelve of the nuptials legitimized children, and three were conducted a few weeks before childbirth. Five marriages legitimized one child each, ranging from two months to thirteen years of age. Three marriages legitimized two children each, one legitimized four, two legitimized six (in both cases the oldest child was thirty-seven), and one couple listed eight children, from ten to twenty-three years old.

During the five year period 1891–1895 following the inauguration of the *Etat civil* in Morne-Paysan, 42 percent of the 231 children born alive were legitimate. By 1957 an additional 10 percent were recorded as legitimate by the marriage of their parents. It is likely that there is some underestimation of later legitimization, since marriages celebrated outside the commune might fail to be noted against the entry of children born within it. This is probable where the parents themselves were born in some other village.

About a third of all children were born legitimate from 1901 to 1923. In 1924, a large-scale campaign by the clergy resulted in a several hundred percent increase in the usual number of marriages (which average normally about five a year, ranging from no marriages in 1921 to eleven in 1941). Most of these mission marriages were celebrated in December, frequently with two and even three weddings on the same day. Many children were legitimized in consequence (ten born in 1921 alone), and in the years following children born legitimate accounted for between half and two-thirds of all live births.

Consensual coresidence as an alternative to marriage is not available to all persons in the village. Women of high socioeconomic status may not live *en ménage.* If they are unable to marry, they must remain childless spinsters. Several village women are in this position. Light-skinned, wealthy, and relatively well-educated, they were left in control of large parcels of land when their brothers became business and professional men in the city and in France. There are no men of comparable position for them to marry within the village. Almost all of them are schoolteachers and active in church-associated works, particularly the Legion of Mary, a lay group which visits and exhorts couples who live consensually to marry. The clergy support the Legion by excluding *ménage* couples from the sacrament of communion and by denying their serving as godparents. The priests frequently preach about the evils of concubinage, and all people agree that from a religious point of view marriage is preferable to consensual cohabitation. A favorite toast at the reception following the baptism of an illegitimate child is, *et que le prochain soit légitime* (may the next one be legitimate). A *ménage* couple who plan to marry, speak of regularizing their relationship. On the other hand, people strongly resent direct clerical interference or what they consider undue pressure. A well-known and well-liked man in a neighboring village died suddenly at a cock fight on a Sunday morning. The clergy refused him a religious burial on the grounds that he was consensually wed. And they made a special point of interpreting his death as divine retribution for attending the cock pit instead of the mass. The men of the village responded by rounding up every vehicle they could find, including the buses which ordinarily are not used on Sunday, and attended the funeral. Many commented that the priest spoke in bad taste because the man was already dead. They found the clergy particularly at fault in refusing to bury him, since they were then denying him any possibility of salvation. Even some ordinarily sympathetic to the priests were critical.

Both men and women agree that in most cases the woman would marry if her mate were willing, although there are some women who prefer what they call the independence of consensual cohabitation. Inability to afford the wedding reception is the most frequently cited reason for not marrying. Others claim that women who are docile and self-effacing while *en ménage,* become arrogant and demanding when married. Stories abound about ideal conjugal relationships which became spoiled upon marriage. "*Un beau ménage,*" goes one non sequitur, "*est mieux qu'un mauvais mariage*" ("Better a happy consensual relationship than a poor marriage"). Even the village priest told me confidentially that married women torment their husbands. He told the story of a couple who had been happily *en ménage* for twelve years and were persuaded to regularize their relationship. After the ceremony the man was seen running out of the church, his face scratched and bleeding, chased by his wife screaming, "At last, you miserable so-and-so!" Musing about the kind of woman that makes the best wife, men speak of a good cook, who does laundry and sews, keeps the house clean, and does not nag. Whatever specifically motivates an individual to marry, it is clear that consensual cohabitation, though it may and frequently does last years, is thought to be less permanent, less committing, than marriage. Both men and women speak of the freedom to terminate a consensually-based *ménage,* a freedom not easily available to married couples. Divorce is extremely rare, as might be expected in so Catholic an area; there are only two divorced women in the village, both consensually remarried. A few married persons are separated, usually older people living alone. On the other hand, many people go through a series of consensual matings. It is not uncommon for a woman to have children from two or three previous *ménages* in addition to those from her current one. Almost a fourth of all children under twenty-four years of age live with their mothers apart from their fathers. A few of these mothers are widows, and one is separated from her husband.

The households of married persons tend to have a simpler structure than do those of consensually wed couples. While married persons may live with their children and sometimes their grandchildren, the households of couples *en ménage* often include collateral kin as well.

Given the possibility of sexual coresidence and childbearing without marriage, why do most people eventually wed? For some, responding to years of pressure from the church and the fear of death, it is a religious act, making of their union one more acceptable to God. Nuptials *in extremis* are celebrated in the home of an elderly, or sick man. Some people marry to assure that their children will inherit, fearing that the state will otherwise take their property. French law recognizes three categories of children: (1) *enfant légitime*—born of married parents or of parents who subsequently marry and declare him as their child. A legitimate child has full rights of inheritance; (2) *enfant reconnu*—born of unmarried parents, but recognized formally by some man and given his name. Recognition can occur at any time after birth. A recognized child is disadvantaged in inheritance if there are legitimate heirs as well, since he is then entitled to only half or less of what he would have received had he been legitimate. The notaries who record property transfers assure that the Napoleonic Code is followed; (3) *enfant naturel*—born of unmarried parents and unrecognized. Such a child has no rights of inheritance from his father. This does not mean that he has no sociological father; his parents may be consensually wed, but his father is unwilling or unable (if, for example, he is already married and living adulterously) to have himself declared the legal father.

Some men hold out the promise of later recognition or legitimization to assure the loyalty and attention of their children. Of twenty-three *enfants naturels* born in 1895, eight were later recognized or legitimized in from five to twenty-three years. The man recognizing the child is not necessarily thought to be the biological father, and there is a case of a girl who having been recognized when she was twenty-one years old, had the recognition annulled fourteen years later in order to marry her former half brother. The court ruled that she could once again carry her mother's name.

Illegitimacy is not normally socially disadvantageous in the village. Many prominent people—the owner of the largest store, the bus driver, members of the municipal council—are illegitimate. Indeed, the three wealthiest families were founded in the late nineteenth century by the natural children of white fathers and creole mothers. The fathers, later married to white women, transferred land to their illegitimate children by making out false acts of sale which were recorded by a notary. Where their fathers live with them, the relationships between illegitimate children and their parents do not seem to be different from those in legally established families. Sometimes these relationships are very intense. The father of a young schoolteacher has been prevented from recognizing his daughter by his hyper-respectable spinster sisters, who claim that their position would be compromised by having official illegitimate children in the family. The girl's mother died when she was three, and she was raised in a different town by another sister of her father. Her father married and has three children. "I *feel* the difference between these three children and me, even though I am older and resemble my father much more than they do. I am not welcome at my aunts' house in Morne-Paysan and am forced to pay my own room and board, when they could so easily take me in. But they are ashamed of me, and don't want me in the house." She and her father still love each other dearly, and she often goes to visit him. The director of the boys' school has two daughters whom he fathered adulterously with a laundress. They can never be legally recognized, but have lived with their father and his wife (whom they call *mamman,* calling their own mother *marraine,* or godmother) all their lives. While they cannot officially inherit more than a small portion which may be reserved for testamentary bequests, he has always seen to their needs, sent them to school, and provided dowries for their weddings.

A child who has neither juridical nor sociological father, for whom no man assumes the role of father, is considered unfortunate. Such a child, technically an *enfant naturel,* is called a *yish korn.* A girl who has such a child, especially if she has more than one, is treated with both pity and contempt. She may have difficulty establishing a durable *ménage* because there are men who refuse to provide for children other than their own. Faced with an ultimatum from a man with whom she would like to live, the mother may send the children to live with her own parents.

On the other hand, recognition does not insure good filial relationships. Some people have nothing to do with their fathers, accusing them of having abandoned their mothers or themselves, or having preferred other children. A constant complaint of old men is that they will be left alone by their children. Mothers seem almost always to retain the loyalty of their children, a fact which seemed to some scholars to imply a continuity with West African polygyny, in which the mother-child unit was the durable one, the father, shared with children of other women, being remote and disinterested. Some women explained their having illegitimate children as a form of old age insurance, guaranteeing that someone will take care of them when they can no longer attract a mate.

The sequence of conjugal relationships—extraresidential mating, consensual cohabitation, and marriage—is characteristic of the peasantry in Martinique, not of the agricultural laborers. Among the laborers marriage is much rarer, and there is evidence that their unions based on consent are much less durable. Some scholars attribute this to the mobility of cane cutters; their travel from plantation to plantation during the harvest for a few days' or weeks' work at each place allows them to establish a rapid series of short-lived liaisons. Most scholars point to the different economic conditions of the two. We have already seen that a woman is an economic necessity to the peasant, since women supervise the marketing of domestically consumed produce. His family is a corporate productive unit, collectively preparing fields, planting, tilling, harvesting, and marketing the crop. The plantation worker contracts individually to sell his labor; economically he gains nothing from marriage. Finally, if marriage is understood as a validation of property holdings, the peasant marries to assure the transfer of his goods to his children; the plantation worker has nothing to transmit. Figures from the Martiniquan census of 1954 clearly show that the percentage of legal unions varies woth control of land:

Occupational Category for Adult Males	*Percent Married*
Landowners	56
Cash renters and sharecroppers	54
Agricultural wage laborers	34

As the agricultural commune with the highest ratio of owners and tenants to salaried farm laborers, Morne-Paysan also has the highest rate of marriage for males and second for females of the thirty-four communes on the island. But the increasing population, the limited and declining amount of land available for peasant cultivation, and its fragmentation each generation are making it difficult for many villagers to maintain themselves as small farmers. Men whose great-grandparents proudly abandoned the estates at emancipation, refusing to cut cane even as paid workers, whose grandparents and parents continued to value their independence from the *habitations* and looked with disdain on those who traveled from estate to estate in search of employment, are now forced to descend to the coastal plains themselves and offer their labor in the sugar fields. No longer able to sustain themselves as yeomen, they are being sucked into the proletariat in the fields, the towns, and along the docks. The change in their economic position will be reflected in their conjugal and familial patterns which increasingly will resemble those of the lowland wage laborers.

If peasantry loses out in Morne-Paysan there will be a corresponding decline in marriage and legitimacy, and an increasing fragility to conjugal relationships. Whether these conditions have their ultimate origin in lower-class European patterns or in a reinterpretation of West African polygyny, or both, it was slavery that caused them to congeal as the characteristic patterns of West Indian domesticity.

Slave owners did not encourage, indeed often prevented, their slaves from marrying. Married or not, the integrity of the conjugal and familial relationships of slaves was violated by the owners who sold children apart from parents, husbands from wives, and assumed ready sexual access to their female slaves. The peasant way of life, which for larger numbers of former slaves became possible at emancipation, provided a new economic system which encouraged an alternative mating pattern, marriage, and durable families. The proletarianization of the peasantry is socially no less than economically a return to the conditions of the plantocracy.

7

The Round of Life: Birth to Death

Birth and Childhood

BELIEFS AND PRACTICES relating to birth are a heritage to rural Latin America from the early *colons* who brought with them an herbal pharmacopoeia and a theory of disease causation and cure as old as Hippocrates. Before the construction of a maternity hospital in St. Pierre in the 1950s, children were born at home, their mothers attended by female neighbors and relatives, and a part-time midwife. (There were no licensed professional *sage-femmes* in the village.) During pregnancy and while nursing the mother follows a special diet, avoiding foods thought to be too "cold" for the intestines, such as avocado, banana, breadfruit and sweet potato which are supposed to cause gas, and pork which causes diarrhea. There is widespread belief that the mother's yearnings and strange, sudden sights are physically manifest as markings on the child's body. A child born polydactyl, or enclosed in a membraneous caul, is said to have the ability to recognize evil spirits and to be protected from them. The midwife burns the membrane, mixes the ashes with a bit of its mother's colostrum, and feeds it to the baby. Until the establishment of the maternity hospital and pre- and postnatal medical visits in the village, the high rate of still births (about 10 percent of all births) and mortality in the first year reflected the lack of effective sanitary conditions. Village women tend to have large families, and more than half the mothers have four or more children.

The mean number of children per mother is 5.2. Information from post-menopausal women shows that married mothers average almost one more child (5.6), than unmarried mothers (4.7), even though they begin having children about a year later.

There is no systematic practice of birth control in the village. Church and State combine to prevent contraceptive information and devices from being dis-

TABLE 14

MEAN AGE FOR FIRST DELIVERIES

Mothers who are married or subsequently marry	21.9 years
Unmarried mothers	20.7 years
All mothers	21.6 years

tributed; the former because of Catholic hostility to artificial interference with procreation, and the latter to reverse the decline in the birth rate in the metropole. Some women are aware of the possibility of limiting conception but do not know how to do it. There is little doubt that many would like to. Many villagers seemed to pity us for not having children, sure that there was some organic reason preventing it. But some sensed that we were privy to knowledge denied them, and several women, individually, came to my wife for information. The conspiracy was not only against the Church but also their husbands. They could assume no cooperation from them, and preferred that their husbands not even know about it. One young couple were working together. They had had five children in as many years, starting when she was sixteen. Her husband had somehow acquired oral contraceptives made in England and smuggled into the island, but they did not know how to use them.

Children are usually named for the saint on whose day they were born. They are rarely named after their parents, although occasionally an *enfant naturel* is given his father's first name. Nicknames, accorded in childhood, last throughout life, and a man's neighbors may be ignorant of his official Christian names. Some sobriquets are contractions or diminutives for the true name, such as 'ti Popo for Hippolyte. While pet animals, particularly horses and dogs, may be named, they are never given human names. (Villagers were shocked that we had named our goats after real people. They said any person would be insulted hearing an animal called by his own name. They were right.) All children are baptised in the church. The child is attended by his godparents and the *da,* a woman who holds him during the ceremony. The parents usually do not come to the church, but receive the godparents and the *da* at home after the ceremony. Godparents are selected from persons whose conjugal status is acceptable to the priest. They are usually not married to each other. Sometimes an uncle or aunt or even an older sibling is chosen, but more frequently the godparents are not closely related to the child. Godparenthood does establish certain relationships between them and the child, and with the child's parents. French terminology is used: the child calls his godfather *parrain* and his godmother *marraine* and his parents call them *compère* and *commère* respectively. These relationships taboo sexual intimacy, and the taboo extends to the children of the godparents. From the point of view of the Church, the godparents are supposed to oversee the religious upbringing of their godchildren. To most of the poorer people in the village, godparents are expected to assist their godchildren materially, and the godparents are frequently chosen from persons economically superior to the child's family. The *compère* should also help his godchild's father. One family complained bitterly when the mayor, godfather to the youngest child, did not choose one of them for road work. Some villagers say that children ought to mourn their godparents as they would their own parents, and godparents should mourn their godchildren. They are less clear on the mourning the death of a *compère* or *commère,* but feel that some demonstration of the loss is in order.

Beyond baptism, there is little ceremonial for children until their First Communion at about seven years of age, when the godparents should provide the requisite dress. A girl's ears are pierced before she begins to teethe, roughly at six months, except that operation is not done during the dry *carême* or *saison des prunes* (April to June) to avoid a plum-like growth which is supposed then to develop in the lobe. Boys who have "good" hair, that is, long and straight, do not have it cut before starting school, and some wear it down to the shoulders. Since small boys and girls dress alike, wearing only a shirt stopping halfway from the waist to the knees, with boys having hair as long as girls, we learned to distinguish them by looking first at the ears. Girls wore either earrings or a circle of string to keep the hole from resealing.

The youngest child is the family pet, pampered and fussed over. We were talking with Madame Félix, as she was nursing her baby Justin, six months old. Her two-year-old, Popo, started to annoy the baby, as he often does when his mother is nursing or playing with him. Mme. Félix told Popo to leave him alone. Five year old Mireille, sitting with a friend, took a burlap sack from Popo. He began to cry, and Mme. Félix told Mireille to give him back the sack, and she would get her one from another room. Mireille did so and then began to cry, and refused to get the other sack. Popo put both his feet in the sack and hopped around. Mireille grabbed it by the bottom, so that Popo fell, hitting his head a bit, and he began to cry again. Mme. Félix hit Mireille several times, and she began to cry, and crawled under a table. Mme. Félix took both the sacks and comforted the crying Popo by letting him crawl up on her lap while she was nursing Justin. Thus each child is expected to be solicitous of the younger ones, and Mme. Félix was as strict with Mireille for teasing Popo as she was with Popo for teasing Justin.

Mothers nurse their children on demand, although they have no objection to giving the child a bottle, now that powdered milk is distributed free to families with infant children. Most children are weaned when about a year old, but with great variation; some are weaned by three months and some continue to nurse for two or three years. Some psychiatrists at the Departmental Mental Hospital, Colson believe that weaning is abrupt and brutal, and attribute instable conjugality to this. In his sexual liaisons, they claim, the man is trying to reestablish the mother-child relationship which was severed when he was weaned. By having a series of these liaisons he reduces the risk of being totally abandoned again, and displaces his aggression against his mother by being unfaithful to his mate. At least in Morne-Paysan, weaning seems not to be generally abrupt, and mothers continue to be affectionate to their weaned children. Indeed it would seem that the Oedipal trauma is reduced in a matrifocal household in which the adult male does not have a great deal of authority over the children.

Few parents seem to worry about toilet-training or teaching children to keep themselves clean. But all parents insist on politeness. Children are taught to shake hands with adults, to say good morning, and not to intrude needlessly on adult conversations. The most insulting thing to say to or about a child is that he is *mal élevé,* badly brought up. Children accuse each other of being *mal élevé* or *sauvage.* We never saw children fighting each other. Almost any adult may ask a child to do anything—fetch water, carry a parcel to the store—and the child obeys quickly and cheerfully. They have very few manufactured toys, and make most of the things they play with. Hoops made from barrels or old bike tire rims are the most popular with younger boys, who roll them down hills guided by a piece of wood or scrap metal. During the season children make rolling toys out of two oranges, fastened together with a piece of wood which serves as an axle. Boys also make tops out of a piece of wood with a nail in the end. Girls jump rope made of vines; the girl who stops the rope by missing a skip changes places with one of the girls who turns. Boys play soccer, the national sport. Teenagers have a real soccer ball and especially during summer when they are on vacation from school in Covin or Fort-de-France they meet to play on a regular terrain. Younger boys kick anything, from a small ball to a coconut or even a stone, playing barefoot on the unpaved road of the town. There are no formal teams in the village for either soccer or track, but a few boys are members of a track team in a nearby town. Children seem rarely to play pretend games in groups; only once in two years did we see some little girls playing school, giggling and trying to look timid as an older girl brandished a stick at them, yelling in a severe voice, "You sit there!"

Much of children's time is spent helping their parents. Toddlers follow older children bringing water from the fountains to the house, and each child carries on his head a can proportional to his size, from little cans about the size of frozen orange juice containers to the large buckets carried by ten-year-old girls. School-age children help clean house and take care of smaller siblings and animals. During planting and harvesting they help cultivate, and daily bring lunch to their fathers in the fields. By the time a boy is ten years old he is proficient with the hoe and machete.

Schooling in Morne-Paysan is limited to the elementary grades. The parish church runs a little nursery school for children of working mothers, supervised by two nuns. The public elementary schools, one each for boys and girls, award the *Certificat d'Etudes* which, in principle, is open to children up to sixteen years old. Because of a shortage of teachers and classrooms, they in fact are closed to children over fourteen. There are enough classes to insure that almost every child in the village has the rudiments of literacy before leaving school. The most difficult year is the first one, when five-year-olds, who have never spoken French, are forced into a situation in which Creole is forbidden. The refusal to permit youngsters to speak Creole is not, interestingly, a decision of the Education Ministry, but of the local teachers who are 100 percent fluent in both languages. Educated and middle-class Martiniquans have been ashamed of Creole, referring to it as broken French (*le français déformé*). I have heard quite dark-skinned parents admonish their children speaking Creole, saying "*Tu parles comme un nègre*" ("You speak like a Negro"). (In the past few years there has been a perceptible change in attitude toward the language, particularly among professional persons of color. A Martiniquan nationalism has developed, related to the rise of independent Africa and *négritude,* which,

Village children. Each morning, children gather vines for the rabbits, whose hutches are shown in the right background.

for a few of its enthusiasts, includes linguistic nativism. Similar nativistic attempts were made unsuccessfully in Ireland and Brittany, with the effort to establish Erse and Breton respectively as languages of normal communication, and successfully with Hebrew in Israel.)

Children attend school every day except Thursday and Sunday. Many receive a meal in the school canteen, while others either bring their lunch or buy *dix francs pain* at the grocery, a piece of a long loaf of bread with a daub of margarine, costing about 2 cents.

A number of children continue on to secondary school at *Cours Complimentaire* in Covin, whose graduates may teach in the elementary schools. A handful each year are admitted to the Lycées in Fort-de-France, to spend six or seven years preparing for the baccalaureate examinations which permit entry to metropolitan universities. Those who pass the exams do not return to the village, and many indeed do not remain in Martinique. While its educational shortcomings are serious, Martinique has enjoyed perhaps the best and most extensive school system within the French overseas world, and Martiniquans have for years gone to France to study law, medicine, and other professions. (There are probably more Martiniquan professionals in France than French professionals in Martinique.) Lycée students who fail the "bacc" still are eligible to compete in examinations for civil service positions, which also enable them to leave the island. Martiniquans have long been prominent in French colonial administration, particularly in West and Equatorial Africa, and to a lesser extent in Southeast Asia. Even today, with Africa independent, one meets Martiniquans and Guadeloupians working for the governments of Niger, the Ivory Coast, and the Upper Volta. Despite the wide distribution of Martiniquans and the awareness of the rest of the French-speaking world, people in the village who have not been in the army overseas have only the vaguest notions of geography. The United States, for many, is a large island just north of Dominica.

No effort is made formally to instruct children about sex, nor is there any serious attempt to shield them from it. Men fondle the penises of little boys, remarking publicly on their size and potential, impressing on the children expectations of their masculinity. Little girls, on the other hand, are supposed to be modest and, although both preschool girls and boys often wear no clothing over their genitals, girls are expected to tug on their shirts to keep from being too easily exposed. Men joke with each other and with boys about their sexuality, pointing with admiration to the sexual organ of a stallion or large dog, and accuse each other of impotence. Women listen smilingly, but do not often interject, except to chase children away if the conversation seems to be getting too bold. Children early learn about sexual intercourse since they sleep in the same room as their parents, and the baby and one or two others may sleep in their parents' bed. Actual sexual experience rarely begins earlier than during the middle and late teens. Young men and women agreed that it is unusual to remain a virgin after seventeen. The most precocious recorded childbirth in the village occurred in 1898, when a boy was born to a thirteen-year-old. On January 3, 1931, both mother and son were married; she for the first time, and he, a widower, for the second.

Adolescence and Adulthood

Girls are given no information about menstruation. One village woman, Lucie, told us that she had been completely unprepared when she had her first menses at thirteen. Her mother told her it was a sore, but at the same time admonished her no longer to play with boys. Her mother died shortly after, and Lucie was raised by her maternal grandmother, who also would not let her be alone with boys. At seventeen she was studying to be a seamstress, going several times a week to St. Pierre, taking her meals at the home of her female cousin. There was to be a ball which she wanted to attend, and Lucie told the grandmother that buses were not returning from St. Pierre that afternoon, and she would stay with her cousin and return the next day. That night they went to the dance, and later to the room of some young men who were living alone, where she had her first sexual experience. She did not like that boy, and never went with him again. During the rest of her seventeenth year she had sexual relations with a young man from Morne-Paysan, whom she had known and liked since they were in school together. Since she was still living with her grandmother they met clandestinely, in the woods near the stream where she did the laundry. She married a man from another commune the next year, and after having one child they separated. As a Catholic she is reluctant to divorce him. At thirty-seven she began an affair with a married man from Fort-de-France; she wants very much to have a child with him, and he has promised her a regular allowance if she conceives.

Most girls have their first affairs with boys from the village, and most conjugal relationships are endogamous. A girl may have sexual intercourse with a number of boys, but once pregnant and *en ménage* she is supposed to remain faithful to her lover. Men, on the other hand, may keep mistresses and several prominent village men are quite open about their extramarital affairs. Women with errant lovers have recourse both to charms and incantations to present themselves in a favorable light, and curses to inflict harm on their rivals. The school director's wife had elephantiasis, called *gros pied* (big foot), which was believed caused by the laundress who had two children with him. Revert, who studied Martiniquan folklore when he was head of the colonial school system, published a notebook seized from a sorcerer which specifies formulas for making oneself loved, causing a woman to come to one's house, and other kinds of love magic (1951:70–74, and *passim*).

Men living consensually or married may have extraresidential affairs, but formal polygyny, in the sense of joint residence, does not exist. *Combosse* refers to two women who are rivals for the same man. It also implies a condition of equivalent status; a woman explained why she didn't visit a neighbor, saying *"i pa combosse mwê"* ("she is not my equal"). The absence of polygynous households has led some scholars to doubt the suggestion that Caribbean conjugal patterns represent a reinterpretation of West African domestic structures.

There appeared to be no homosexual establishments in the village during our stay, but people did recall two men who long ago lived conjugally. These *zami* (that is, friends, a euphemism for homosexual or *macommére*), we are told, repented of their behavior before death, and "made peace with the church." All denied that carnal relations with animals was known in Martinique. One man suggested that such behavior was more likely *en métropole,* that is, in France.

The ethos of friendship and sociability is invoked to regulate social interrelationships within the village. People of Morne-Paysan are friendly, we are told, different from the people of such-and-such a place who are self-centered (*égoïste*) as well as black. "We never visit Precheur," a neighbor remarked, "because they're all as black as pigs." "In Morne-Paysan," another commented, "we are all one family" (*"les voisins sont des parents"*). There is a great deal of visiting, dropping in unannounced upon a friend or relative. Whenever adults visit they are received warmly, invited inside, and offered something to drink. All people have a tray and a few nice glasses for welcoming visitors. If there is nothing in the house to serve, a child is sent to the store to buy some rum, wine, beer, or soda. In a very poor house, where the host cannot afford even that, a child is sent scampering up a coconut palm to throw down some green nuts. The host whacks an opening with a blow of his machete, and the fresh milk is served in glasses. In season, orange juice is served. Fruit or roasted nuts are served during the visit, and the guest may not leave without taking with him a large quantity of oranges or mangoes, or a stem of bananas. Gift-giving is expected to be reciprocal, but need not be equivalent. A woman gave a poorer neighbor a dress she no longer wanted to wear. A few days later, she received a cold baked sweet potato. Gifts of food or flowers may be given as apologies as well as for thanks.

Men usually meet their friends in bars after working in the fields. Each man who enters makes a tour of the room, shaking hands with everyone there, even with strangers. The men drink a local version of the *petit punch,* the national beverage: raw white rum, with *sirop* (boiled sugar water) and flavored with a piece of lime peel, swallowed in a gulp and chased with a glass of water. In all the rural bars a bottle of rum, a bowl of sugar, and a water caraffe are left on each table. No one watches the amount of rum in a drink nor how many drinks a man has. Each pays when he leaves, giving the owner about 10 cents for each glass. Farming and politics are the invariable topics of conversation. The village has been deeply rent by politics (see Chapter 8), and men vigorously discuss local affairs as well as international happenings, which they learn about in the press and from village politicians. There is great admiration for men who are able to speak French eloquently and with humor. The men are always delighted with mimicry. The mayor and the priest are principal targets, both given to pompous, long-winded speeches, readily parodied before an appreciative audience. Even members of the incumbent party respond happily to ridicule of their leaders.

Most of the bars are politically neutral (although their owners are associated with one or the other side). Politics has affected visiting people at home. The mayor was a Gaullist, the opposition were Socialists. Men out of sympathy with the mayor and the municipal government frequently got together at the school director's house, to play dominoes, talk, and listen to him discuss politics. The director is an elderly man, very tall, one of two whites born in the village, and is married to a colored woman. (The mayor is phenotypically white, but has many colored relatives in the region.)

Women's visiting is more limited since they rarely go out in the evening and go to the bars only to buy food or drink to take home. They visit each other during the day, arranging to give a *coup-de-main* in sewing or shelling peanuts. They often meet at the rivers, where they go to do the laundry, and spend hours exchanging information. Women's talk centers on interpersonal gossip and sickness.

> Did you know that 'Ti Sonson's daughter was pregnant, and the old man threatened to throw her out? Of course he didn't, and even promised to furnish the house when the boy offered to provide a home for them. And Mme. Ste-Marie gave money to the *quimboiseur* from Guadeloupe who told her he had a charm to increase business at her shop. Stupid woman! She should know a Guadeloupian can't be trusted. And old papa Laumire is sick and the children are already arguing about the land. The son in Fort-de-France said if he doesn't get a fair share he'll go to court. He's getting just like city folk, always involving outsiders in family affairs. Not like us who rather lose a bit than make a big fuss. And isn't it terrible how the price of fcod keeps going up? Yes, everything is becoming too dear to live.

Health

An almost obsessive interest in health pervades the thoughts of villagers. At first one accepts the queries about health which are invariable parts of every conversation as mere formulas of etiquette. *Et la santé? Et madame, pas de maladies? Alor, u pa malade?"* ("And your health? Your wife is not sick? You are not sick?") But each query demands an answer, a full account of domestic morbidity since the last time you met. Then you notice how often the state of health is invoked as an explanation for why something did or did not happen, or for the general fatalism about the external world. For example, talking about the war in Algeria (at that time already grim for the French) or about taxes, a villager may state, "*et ka u le, mwê toujours malade*" ("so what do you want, I'm always sick"). Things and activities are evaluated in terms of the contribution they make to health. Thatched roofing on wattle-and-daub huts (called *gaulette* or *case en terre*) was beginning to be replaced in 1957–1958 by corrugated galvanized-iron sheets. Everyone who shifted to metal justified the move as requiring less upkeep, but inevitably added that thatch is better for the health. (By 1964 there were no thatched roofs left, and there remained just a dozen or so *gaulettes* not yet replaced by cement bricks.)

Their obsession with sickness is all the more curious in view of their conviction that Morne-Paysan, by virtue of its climate and altitude, is the healthiest commune on the island, and point to individuals of remarkable longevity as evidence. It is true that several villagers were over ninety, and many were in their seventies and eighties. Mortality is highly bimodal by age; a fifth of all deaths (excluding stillbirths) occurs in the first year of life, and an additional 15 percent before the tenth year. A third live to the age of sixty or more.

There are serious health problems in the village, deriving from the lack of

TABLE 15

Age at Death	Percent of Total
0–1	20.6
1–9	15.3
10–19	2.9
20–29	2.4
30–39	8.2
40–49	7.6
50–59	10.0
60–6o	11.8
70–79	15.3
80+	5.9
TOTAL	100.0

sanitary sewage and fresh-water facilities. The arid southern part of Martinique receives its water from a purification station just above the capital city. The north, however, is generally well watered and crisscrossed with streams running from the Pitons du Covin which enjoy over 5 meters of rainfall annually (as contrasted with 1½ meters or less along the southern coast). These streams are infested with dysentery and snails which host intestinal parasites causing schistosomiasis. There is no cure and as yet no prevention other than guaranteeing uncontaminated water supplies, as people do laundry, bathe, and clean chamber pots in the same streams from which they get their drinking water. Everyone in the village has these *vers* (worms), and they have various herbal concoctions which are supposed to relieve them. Beyond schistosomiasis, the major complaint is malnutrition, particularly as it affects the teeth. According to Dr. H. Perronnette (1963:64) of the *Centre Départmental d'Education Sanitaire, Démographique, et Social,* 70 percent of all children from two to four years of age suffer from diseases caused by malnutrition, which he attributes not to the absence of nutritional foods but to their poor utilization. The other chronic, not immediately incapacitating diseases which visit the Martiniquan countryside are leprosy and elephantiasis. A branch of Institut Pasteur has been established in Martinique which has facilities for research and treatment of these peculiarly tropical ailments. Malaria, which used to be endemic in the island, has been almost entirely eradicated through a vigorous program of mosquito control. Finally, alcoholism and alcoholic deterioration are serious problems in Martinique; more than a fifth of the female patients and a third of the males admitted to the psychiatric hospital at Colson suffer from delirium tremens. (The psychiatrists attributed this to a fantastic search for the maternal protection lost at weaning.)

Villagers maintain a dualistic theory of the causation of disease. They explain certain ailments by the action of natural events. They have some notion of the germ theory, and speak of *microbes* which cannot be seen and yet which enter the body, multiply, and do harm. They recognize the vulnerability of the very young and the very old, especially to infection; they know they are supposed to wash their hands before feeding the baby. They understand accidents, and are quick to wash out a machete wound and to request a tetanus shot from the nurse. They also believe that illness may be the result of nonnatural events and that the two may be combined. That a wound from a machete may become infected because of germs is readily accepted. But this does not explain why a particular person was wounded, or who caused him to swing the machete in such a fateful way. The evil eye (*mal jeu*), sorcery (*quimbois*), the devil (*diable*), and his agents (*zombis* and *engagés*) are the ultimate sources of evil, including illness.

This duality has been reported by scholars working in peasant villages in various parts of Central and South America and in India. It is interesting that in Martinique it is shared by a large part of the professional medical corps, that is, persons whose primary identification is with modern scientific medical practices. The late Professor Alfred Métraux, Dr. Jean Benoist, and I attended a meeting at the psychiatric hospital at Colson, which was held to discuss possible connections between mental illness and beliefs about the supernatural. We had asked the psychiatric nurses whether any of their patients believed they were in the hospital because of the actions of a sorcerer, or the like. One of the nurses immediately responded that when she was on duty at another hospital, a woman was brought in who had no skin. The patient was an *engagé,* a person who has made a pact with the devil and, in exchange for his soul, is given certain powers. She had the power to become an animal, and was marauding about the countryside in this form when someone discovered her empty skin which she had neglected to conceal. Realizing what he had, the discoverer liberally doused the skin with spices, and the *engagé* was unable to put it back on. She took ill and was brought to the hospital. Thus the nurse explained an unusual depigmentation or perhaps drug-induced exfoliation of skin in a culturally reasonable way. The other nurses listening asked her if she wasn't frightened. No, she explained, she was born *coiffée,* therefore protected. (This is a variant of the *loup-garou* [werewolf] story, brought to the West Indies from Europe. Simpson [1942] collected many of them in Haiti.)

There is a public nurse in Morne-Paysan, Mlle. Justine, who has a small dispensary in the bourg. Her job is to assist the government doctor who comes once a week to examine infants and pregnant and postpartum women; to make rounds of the *quartiers,* visiting the sick and carrying out instructions from a doctor (such as injections); and handling emergencies. She is an enormous, square, rock-like woman, with gray eyes, very light skin, and iron gray hair always tightly wound in little mounds on her head. Although she has visited France and is fluent in French, she is comfortable only in Creole. Only when the doctor is in the dispensary does she speak French. While he is there she struts about busily, imperiously instructing the women to keep still; as soon as he leaves, everyone relaxes, and she speaks no more French for another week. But she never stops talking; apparently, even when she's alone (she's a spinster) she talks to herself or to her animals. When she leaves you, after politely shaking hands and saying goodbye, she continues her monologue, turning her back on you, walking slowly away, speaking now to a tree, now to a rock, gesticulating grandly at some particularly dramatic point.

Mlle. Justine believes fervently in the supernatural. "*Médecins rient, mais mwé ka du . . .*" ("Doctors laugh, but *I* tell you . . ."), she says repeatedly. She has an extensive knowledge of herbal medicine. I once accompanied her as she went on rounds, and every so often she would dart off the path to pick a leaf or stem of a plant she spotted in a field. Visiting a patient, she administered the medicine or injection prescribed by a physician, and then prepared a tea from the herbs she had just gathered. At the dispensary she freely prescribes herbal remedies, and was an endless source of information about them. Mlle. Justine could tell when some one was really sick, and was big and loud enough to force him to visit the doctor.

Everyone in the village knows something about herbal medicine. Even little children are sent out in the fields to collect plants and are told how to prepare them. The local pharmacopoeia is, for the most part, a heritage from Europe, with the addition of plants native to the island. Most of them now grow wild, and are gathered in the fields, but a few are intentionally cultivated, usually in a little garden near the house. We collected more than a hundred plants, the most prominent of which are the following:

Corossol (Annona muricata). Used as an infusion for intestinal parasites and as a sedative. It is also used as a topical wash for babies who are nervous or convulsive.
Zeb à cornettes (Borreria laevis) An infusion to promote blood circulation and to cure the common cold.
Thé pays (Capraria biflora). This is cultivated and made into a tea used externally for ailments of the eye and internally for the blood and liver. It is also supposed to be a diuretic.
Zeb à vers (Chenopodium ambrosioides). Infusion for intestinal parasites.
Zeb à chatte (Hebiclinium macrophyllum ?) Infusion for pregnant women with stomachache.
Marie derrière l'hôpital (Lantana camara). Tea made of the flowers to reduce hypertension.
Pompom soldat (Leonotis nepetaefolia). Infusion to reduce fever.
Veronique (Lindernia diffusa). Infusion for coughs. It is reputed to be used against leprosy, but we have no firsthand testimonial.
Racquette (Opuntia dillenii). This cactus is cultivated for its thick leaves, which are grated and cooked with manioc flour, and applied as a poultice for abcesses.
Mouron calebasse (Peperomia rotundifolia). This is a topical stimulant, mixed with rum and rubbed on rheumatic hands and on fighting cocks.
Plaintin (Plantago major). Liquid is extracted from the leaves by pressing or applying heat with an iron. The liquid is used topically in the eyes and the leaves are used directly on open sores.
Verveine (Stachytarpheta jamaicensis). The plant is allowed to stand in water for several hours, after which the water is drunk as a diuretic and for internal inflammation and indigestion.
Menthe glaciale (Tanacetum vulgare). This plant is cultivated in Morne-Paysan, and made into an infusion drunk to aid digestion and to relieve hernia.

Villagers also use patent medicines and aspirin, and commercially prepared tonics, labelled *elixir de santé* (elixir of health) or *cologne de vie* (life cologne). These can be bought in grocery stores and in the markets. In the large markets some women specialize in herbal and patent medicines, crying out that they sell *'potek créole.* Even the professional pharmacists trade in local herbs, and many compound special packets of leaves and roots labelled "for the blood," or "for the liver." Martiniquans seem to have inherited from the French peculiarly sensitive livers, and they complain of ailments referred to as *foie colonial* and *foie tropique* (colonial and tropical liver).

The nurse is the only representative of scientific medical practice resident in Morne-Paysan. St. Pierre, some 8 kilometers distant, is the nearest place where there is a doctor and pharmacist (other than the TB sanatarium near Covin). A government physician visits the village once a week or once every two weeks to examine infants and mothers; he is not available for general medicine. When a physician is needed urgently such as for a machete wound, the patient usually must be brought to him, for the doctors are unwilling to risk their cars over the rough unpaved road. The commune owns a jeep operated by the mayor which is supposed to be used to transport persons to doctors or to the hospital. Often the mayor is unavailable, since he uses the jeep as his personal car, or the patient is identified with the political opposition and unwilling to ask the mayor for help. In 1957–1958 there was another car, owned by a shopkeeper, which could be rented for trips. A neighbor told me that her son had cut his foot badly while working in the garden, and since she could find neither the mayor, nor the shopkeeper, nor me, she borrowed a horse, put her son in the saddle, and walked to St. Pierre and back. The round trip took seven hours.

Once when I was making rounds with the nurse, she asked the mayor to transport a sick woman to St. Pierre. He refused, saying he needed the car for road work; men were blasting rocks with dynamite, using the battery for contact. He told the nurse to phone the doctor instead, describe the ailment, and have him call a prescription into the pharmacist. Then someone could take the bus later in the day and pick up the medication.

It would be wrong to account for the tenacity of traditional medicine on the grounds that it is less expensive than scientific practice. There are doctors in Martinique whose fees are high, and many doctors demand at least part payment prior to an examination. This has caused serious resentment at least in one case when the physician upon looking at the patient recommended immediate removal to the hospital. The patient felt that the doctor had done nothing to merit payment. Yet in Martinique most rural people can have their medical and pharmaceutical expenses covered by *Assistance médicale gratuite,* a form of social security, and continue to visit folk practitioners whose bills are not honored by the government.

Folk or traditional medical practitioners are collectively called *guérisseurs* (curers). Most of these are villagers, particularly knowledgable about herbal remedies or adept at curing specific ailments. They rarely charge for their services, at least not to other villagers, although they are compensated by gifts. When I was ill for a while in 1957 (the nurse diagnosed my case as malaria with yellow fever, and harangued my wife for having delayed so long notifying the carpenter since he would have scarcely enough time to make the coffin), neighbors visiting often suggested infusions and *tisanes,* and warned me about foods I had to avoid on pain of immediate demise (eggs and cacao were especially suspect). Neighbors were also helpful in prescribing relief for diarrhea: chop together young guava leaves and two small chunks of burnt toast; steep in boiling water ten or fifteen minutes, strain, and drink with or without sugar.

Midwives are the most specialized local *guérisseurs.* Since the construction of the maternity hospital in St. Pierre, most children are no longer born in the village. But some women, particularly those with large families, prefer to have their children at home, assisted by a neighbor. Even women who prefer to deliver in the hospital frequently find themselves unable to arrange transportation. We were sitting in a bar chatting when a young woman, extremely pregnant, came jauntily walking by. *"Sa ka commencé?"* ("It's beginning?" that is, labor) she was asked. "Yes," she responded, in high spirits, and was prepared to walk all the way to St. Pierre.

Other curers combine a knowledge of herbal remedies with familiarity with the supernatural. Martiniquans believe that disease may be supernaturally caused; it is only logical, therefore, to believe that an effective cure can come only from someone who is able to manipulate that supernatural.

To a great extent, this attitude is encouraged by the Church. People who are ill direct their prayers to St. Anthony, whose statue is just inside the church entrance. All around the statue are carved marble votive plaques, recording the gratitude of the petitioner for having been cured. Most say merely *Grace à St. Antoine* (thank you, St. Anthony), while others go to some length describing the ailment removed from them. Certain priests are known to be miracle workers. Some villagers used to go to a Canadian missionary. We were told of one villager who came to him with a huge, swollen black-as-charcoal leg, caused by another man. This enemy had gone to a powerful *quimboiseur* and paid him to cause an avalanche as the villager was walking along. A rock hit his leg, breaking it in many places. The man had spent three months in the hospital to no avail. Finally he went to the priest, who cured him immediately.

People claimed that the bishop wanted to defrock the priest, but he threatened to reveal all the priests' secrets, so he was left alone. He was able to sense evil without having to see it. Once, we were told, he went to Fonds Capot, the fishing village near Morne-Paysan. He knocked at a house and asked to come in. Through the closed door, a woman refused. He broke through the door, and found a skull and a burning candle on the table, which he threw out into the sea.

Many colored Martiniquans seek the assistance of the East Indian priests or *l'abbé coolies* of the cult of Maldevidan (see Horowitz 1963; Horowitz and Klass 1961). These men do not claim to be able to cure, themselves, being merely intermediaries between the supplicant and the deities. During ceremonials held in the courtyards of the seven Hindu temples, the priest standing barefoot on freshly sharpened machetes is possessed by a god. Through the mouth of the priest the god answers questions, explains what caused an illness and what must be done to be cured. The supplicant shows his gratitude by offering a sheep which is sacrificed by a blow from one of the machetes on which the priest stood. If the head is severed in a single blow the people shout joyously, interpreting this as a sign that the sacrifice has been accepted.

Quimboiseurs may use their powers to heal as well as to harm. Edouard, twenty-nine years old, told me how he suffered unbearably from rheumatism for eight years, often unable to work and hardly able even to feed himself. He had gone to several physicians, who could do nothing for him. Then a few years ago, someone suggested he see Monsieur Bernard, a man who lived in Fort-de-France and had a reputation for curing by *magnetisme*. Edouard went to his home, and before he even described his complaint, Bernard told him why he had come, making an accurate diagnosis. He then asked Edouard the name of his most recently dead male relative and, holding his hand, invoked the presence of a saint. Edouard was unable to hear what the saint said, but Bernard listened intently, writing down the saint's instructions, occasionally asking him to repeat or go a little slower. The treatment involved three visits, and each time Bernard received instructions from the saint. Edouard was ordered to sit on a large vase filled with boiling water for as long as he could tolerate the heat. This was supposed to circulate through the body and unblock the arteries. Bernard also copied down two prescriptions which he gave to Edouard. Edouard told me that this convinced him of Bernard's sincerity, since many of the items had to be bought in a drug store. If he were a charlatan, he would have tried to sell the ingredients himself. The prescriptions are exactly as follows:

1. *comme tisane l'eau bouillir rouge de vin 2 carrotte crage* (as a tea boil water, red wine, and two grated carrots)
   le matin un cuillere Sirop Hemoglobine de chien dan te pache cafe (in the morning take one teaspoon of Hemoglobin Deschiennes in a tea made from ground coffee)
   A 11 un tit vers vin tonique vial, et le soir (at 11 A.M. and in the evening take a small glass of wine)
   pasetille pulmole dan la journez (during the day take cough drops)
   Friction (massage)
   tafia pur 3 tit Sitron 2 miscard, morceau charbon terre. 3 tit tientir Danica (pure white rum, three small limes, two nutmegs, a piece of charcoal. Three drops of arnica)
   puge l'eau de vie almande dan du cafe samas (purge with brandy and coffee)
2. *Bouillir 3 litre D'eau un proien Sel Semdre a maret densin lunge videe denin vase couver d'une laine repliere en d'eau assise dese 15 minuit.* (Boil three liters of water with salt and pour it in a vase covered with a piece of wool. Sit on it for 15 minutes.)
   l'eaux froid et du vinaigre a la bouche en Sotheen 1 soir le deuxieme de meme. le jour sotez fait la meme choses pour le deux pied. 3 pour chaque. (Wash mouth with vinegar and cold water the first and second evenings. During the day do the same to the feet, three times for each.)
   te un feuille guiapenna la peau Sitron canelle morceau feuille mangot vert jeonne quenette jeonne. Cogna un cuillere samas 2 asperine. (Tea made of leaves of various fruit trees, a teaspoon of cognac, and two ground aspirins.)
   un cuillerre poudre charbon pour un litre D'eau plur bouillir coulet un tit vers tout le lonsheu. (A teaspoon of powdered charcoal in a liter of boiled water, poured into a small glass to be taken every day at 11.)
   tisane vichyflort un cuillere pour un litre D'eau bouillir vides desir boir samese. (Tea made of mineral water and water.)

This prescription is a chaotic parody of modern medical practice. The form of the complex series of instructions and large number of medications does not differ greatly from those prescribed by French-trained physicians. One local doctor to whom I showed the prescription remarked that Bernard is either an idiot or extremely intelligent, intentionally misspelling to protect himself from a criminal charge of incompetent prescribing. "Hemoglobin de chien" is not dog's blood, but a preparation from the Deschiennes drug company. In any case, Edouard's cure was complete, and he reports never again to have suffered from rheumatism.

Death

While there has been much scholarly interest in Caribbean marriage, relatively little has been written about the institutionalization of death. This is curious because funerary activities are very important in these islands, and in the rural areas they are occasions of almost total assemblage. Forde (1962:89), discussing mortuary rites among the Yakö of eastern Nigeria, summarizes the anthropological perspective:

> It has been a commonplace since the pioneer studies of Van Gennep, Radcliffe-Brown and Malinowski that the main social significance of such ceremonies, including the provision and transfers of goods and the changes of status associated with them, was to be found in a reaffirmation of the solidarity and a restoration of the structure of social groups that had suffered loss.

In Morne-Paysan, death, particularly of an adult male, has ramifications throughout the highly interdependent population of the village: property must be divided among heirs, involving sometimes half-forgotten or suppressed matters of legitimacy, recognition, and bastardy; a widow and dependent children may have to be cared for; a labor-exchange group may have to find a new member mutually acceptable to the survivors, and so on. The wide and involuted network of kinship within the village means that almost everybody has lost a kinsman to whom a relationship may be demonstrated in several ways.

A special tolling of the parish bells formally apprises the village of a death. In fact it is likely that word has circulated long before the sacristan mounts the belfry stairs. By law, burial follows within twenty-four hours, and the commune has established 5 P.M. of the day following the demise for the actual interment. Plans for the funeral service are made between the priest and the representatives of the religious societies—for example, Scapulary, Legion of Mary—to which the deceased may have belonged. The priest determines the class of funeral the survivors want or will pay for, and inquiries about the dead person's moral life to make certain that religious participation is not precluded.

There are three carpenters in the village, all of whom make unornamented plank-box coffins. They do not stock them already made, explaining they do not have the capital. One of them said that his wife does not permit him to make a coffin in advance, fearing that she would then die. Another said it would look as if he were too anxious to profit from death. The commune pays 7000 francs (about $14) for the coffins of indigents; individuals paying themselves are charged up to 10,000 francs (about $20). A fine coffin requires eight planks, which cost the carpenter about 450 francs each, plus nails and varnish.

The body in its coffin is carried to the church accompanied by all persons whose homes the procession passes. Every household is represented at least by its senior male, who appears solemnly in a black suit, white shirt, and black tie. Many people living in other parts of the island return for the burial, and funeral services are the only church rites that have any substantial male participation. The black-vested priest and his accolytes officiate at the requiem mass. Following the solemn rites the coffin, accompanied by the priest (in the case of a first-class funeral), members of the religious societies aiding the pallbearers, the family, and the other persons of the community, is carried to the graveyard about a half-mile away. There it is placed in the family crypt or in a freshly opened grave. The dead man is eulogized in French, particularly by politicians. The mood is solemn and somber, and the crowd quietly disperses and goes home. According to the procedures of the Roman Catholic Church, requiem masses in honor of the deceased are held from time to time.

The cemetery belongs not to the church but to the commune, which provides the grave diggers. A notice in the town hall announces the prices:

tomb-opening (which may require masonry)	500 francs
gravedigging (child)	300
gravedigging (adult)	500

Again no charge is made for indigents. There are about thirty family tombs, massive masonry structures, each with a small shrine recessed in the cement. A simple wooden cross marks the other graves, and these deteriorate rather quickly. Since the cemetery is quite small, all the available ground has been used, and new graves are opened in the place of old ones, the remaining bones of the former occupants being exposed in the pile of earth. One gravedigger estimated about a fifteen-year cycle of plot reuse.

Children's rites are very simple. Few adults attend. The coffin is carried by little girls, dressed in white, overseen by women from the religious societies. The priest does not accompany the procession to the cemetery, because the child is considered to be without sin, hence does not require elaborate ritual.

The most elaborate ceremony was the burial of a soldier who had been killed in Algeria, whose body was shipped home. Invitations had been printed in advance, with the date penned in. As soon as the body arrived, the funeral was held. The coffin was large, bearing a metal plaque stating that herein lay a soldier who died for his country. The coffin was laid out in the town hall, instead of the church, with a crucifix at the head, candles and flowers along the side, and a wreath against the side. A *tricouleur* was draped across the casket, and the flags in the town hall were bound with black cloth.

In addition to villagers, the funeral was attended by a group of gendarmes and a military honor guard of five soldiers and an officer. The priest was assisted by a colleague who had served the village some years earlier. At the grave side the soldiers stood at attention with shouldered rifles while speeches were made. The first was by an old man who had been a professional soldier, wearing his uniform with a chestload of medals. He spoke simply and briefly about the boy. The second speaker was the president of the *Anciens Combattants de la Deuxième Guerre Mondiale*

(World War II Veterans), who used his platform to denounce the Algerians rebels. A very dark-skinned man, he spoke eloquently about "we Frenchmen" dying at the hands of "ungrateful rebels." Finally the mayor spoke.

When an adult dies, a wake or *veillée* is held the night before the burial. Neighbors wash the body with rum, seal the orifices with small pieces of lime, and force a liter or more of strong rum down the throat as a temporary preservative. The corpse is dressed fully, except for shoes, usually in black if married, otherwise in white, and laid out on a bed, with a pillow under the head and a crucifix in the hand. Candles burn at the head and feet, and a small branch with leaves on it is placed by the shoulder to be used to chase away flies. The coffin is displayed nearby if it has already been acquired. Two glasses are at the foot of the bed, one containing a floating wick burning in oil, the other filled with water and a small sprig of leaves. Close relatives of the deceased sit on chairs along the sides of the room, praying and quietly singing hymns. Each visitor enters the room in turn, sprinkles the body with the sprig, and kneels in prayer. Occasionally a mourner kisses the body. Before leaving, the visitor shakes hands with the seated relatives, offers condolences, and may sit and talk a while. The atmosphere is solemn but rarely is there crying. The behavior in the room containing the deceased and bereaved family seems to anticipate the solemnity of the sacred church rites the following day. There is no priest, but there is prayer leadership, as one woman selects from her missal particular bits of liturgy.

In the yard outside, long benches are set up forming three sides of a square. After leaving the house, the visitors, especially the men, sit on these benches and drink coffee, rum, and water, prepared and served throughout the night. The atmosphere here is noisy and jovial, in contrast to the quiet decorum in the house. A man stands up to lead a song, in which he shouts a line and the others respond. Between verses he dances around the yard, wearing his hat upside down like a buffoon. After each song he yells out this formula, admonishing the crowd to reply together:

Leader: *kri* (Christ?)
Others: *kra*
L: *ekri*
O: *ekra*
L: *e.kri*
O: *e.kra*
L: *antikri*
O: *antikra . . .*

The singing may be interrupted by someone who rises to eulogize the deceased. Another stands to tell a story about *zombis, loups-garous* (werewolves), *guiablesses* (devils), and the like. Under the light of a lantern, some men and children play dominoes. A man announces riddle telling with a loud *titim,* to which the others respond *bois sèche.* They seem to enjoy hearing old riddles as much as new ones.

Q. *dlo môte mô?* (Water goes up a hill?)
R. *koko.* (A coconut.)
Q. *dlo desen mô?* (Water goes down a hill?)
R. *kan.* (Sugarcane.)

Q. *sa de zom ka fe, de fam pa sav fe.* (What two men can do, two women cannot do.) *sa yô om e yô fam ka fe de fam pa sav fe.* (What a man and a woman can do, two women cannot do.)
R. *confession.* (Confession, that is, in church.)
Q. *mwê pase cimetière.* (I passed a cemetery.)
mwê di bonjours. (I said good morning.)
tu mo la repô mwê. (All the dead answered me.)
tu vivâ pa repô mwê. (The living did not answer me.)
R. *pwa sek, paw ver.* (Dried peas, green peas.) When the wind passes over a field no noise is made by the green peas, but the dry peas rattle in the pods.
Q. *wo wo ba ba yê yê.* (High high low low, fruit flies.)
R. *fruit-à-pain.* (Breadfruit.) The fruit is in the tree, then it falls and rots, and is covered with fruit flies.
Q. *mun ki fe mwê, vâ mwê.* (Who made me sold me.)
mun ki ashet mê, pa buzwâ mwê. (Who bought me doesn't need me.)
mun ki buzwâ mwê, pa ka we mwê. (Who needs me doesn't see me.)
R. *cercueil.* (A coffin.)
Q. *yô mamâ kan i fashe, tu yish li byê abiye. Tâdi ki le byê ge, tu yish li tu ni.* (When mother is angry her children are well dressed. When she is happy they are nude.)
R. *rivière.* (River.) When the river is rough, the stones are covered; when it is calm they are exposed.

With the exception of a few who echo the churches' hostility toward the *veillée,* almost all the village adults who are physically able make an appearance, and many stay most of the night, laughing, singing, joking, and telling stories. Young people take the opportunity to rendezvous and quietly disappear into the fields. Revert (1951:33) contrasts the tone in the house with that in the yard:

> *There is the most extraordinary diptych imaginable: around the body, lamentations and the chanting of plaintive verses; outside, at least it seems, the noisiest merry-making.*

The village priest protested to me that he would not lend his presence to petting, dirty stories, and paganism.

This seeming sacred-profane opposition in mortuary rites is reflected in the Martiniquan celebration of carnival. As in other parts of the New World where the French or Iberian tradition is strong, Martinique has a pre-Lenten carnival season, with much dancing, drinking, and masked celebrants roaming about the streets. Martinique is unique in being the only place in the world where carnival continues beyond Mardi Gras to Ash Wednesday. On the day signalling the beginning of Lent, thousands assemble in the savanna of Fort-de-France, starkly costumed in black-and-white (in contrast to the flamboyant colorful robes of the day before), to mourn the death of Carnival itself. Forming a procession they wind through the city, pleading, "*malgre la vie a red/ vaval pa kite nu*" ("even though life is difficult/ do not leave us, Carnival"). Each time the procession passes a church, a small group of Legionnaires led by the priest solemnly protests by breaking through the line of marchers.

In his consideration of death in the Hebrides, Vallee (1955:128) writes: "Mourning and burial rituals provide one of the most frequent occasions upon which community members meet to express their unity and to re-affirm the values upon which that unity is based." If values are reaffirmed by these rites, the opposition between the wake and the burial in Morne-Paysan, an opposition which obtains in almost every element of the obsequies, reflects the complexity of the rural Martiniquan culture which is being upheld.

TABLE 16

OPPOSITION BETWEEN THE WAKE AND THE BURIAL

Wake	Burial
Body exposed on bed	Body concealed in coffin
Place: house and yard	Place: church and cemetery
Time: night	Time: day
Leadership: relatives and neighbors (no priest)	Leadership: priest and religious sodalities
Eschatology: "pagan": *zombis*, *engagés*	Eschatology: "Christian": Christ, Mary, saints
Language: Creole	Language: French and Latin
Liturgy: prayers, eulogies, jokes, songs, riddles, tales	Liturgy: Catholic service; eulogies by politicians
Hospitality: drink, games, intoxication	Hospitality: religious service, sobriety
Tone: somber in house; joyful, spontaneous in yard	Tone: solemn, formal

In short, the priest-church-"Christian"-sober-French-authority set does not exhaust the meaningful world within which the Martiniquan peasant operates. This is a part, a very important part. But the peasant reaffirms also the everyday, mundane, egalitarian sphere in which his house, yard, and fields dominate, in which explanations involving *zombis* and *engagés* are also relevant, and in which Creole, not French, is the language of communication. The wake and the burial are opposed because they appeal to different sets of values.

8

Consensus and Conflict

> Throughout [Plantation-America], there seems to be a weak sense of community cohesion, and local communities are but loosely organized. . . . This lack of community *esprit de corps* is perhaps the reason why so many studies of the Caribbean area are not, in the strict sense of the term, "community studies," and why the community unit remains so vaguely defined (Wagley 1957:8).

This statement does not describe Morne-Paysan. Geographical, political, and sociological factors make the village readily definable, separable from the rest of the countryside. By virtue of the extreme steepness of the mountains to the east there are no houses above 2000 feet, and the lands of villagers do not merge imperceptibly with those of some other village. On the open western side, where the hills are gentler as they descend to the sea, the village is isolated by being off the main road, and reached only by a branch road which was unpaved until 1958.

As we saw in Chapter 3, the highland villagers had long agitated for political separation from coastal Covin, arguing that their devotion to peasant farming left them inadequately represented in the municipal council of that plantation and fishing commune. In 1872, a parish was established in the hills. In 1891, there was an office of the *Etat civil.* And in 1947, the villagers finally won recognition as a commune, with their own mayor and municipal council. They mapped the region themselves, using the Pitons and the plantations to describe the limits. Thus the village is a political entity. It owns a town hall, a cemetery, and several schools. It takes a census and receives revenues.

It is not economically corporate. The village as such does not own or control productive lands nor their exploitation. It does not formally restrict access to productive lands to any specially certified group of persons.

Yet the villagers claim and outsiders acknowledge a difference between them and persons from other parts of the island. The sources of this unity, of the integration of the village, lie in kinship, in religion, in economics, and politics. These institutions organize the villagers cooperatively, creating links of solidarity among them. At the same time, however, these very institutions are sources as well of contention, discord, and schism. In a sense Morne-Paysan may be thought of as having a segmental structure, tending toward unity vis à vis the outside world, and fragmenting internally into competing and opposed sections.

Even for Martinique, Morne-Paysan is a small village. Its population of 1650 persons has scarcely changed over fifty years; 98 percent of its potential increases from declining mortality rates has been offset by a steady emigration to the estates, the city, and overseas. Immigration is minor. Two-thirds of the family names inscribed in the *Etat civil* in 1951 also appear in the registry for 1891–1895. Very few persons from other parts of the island have established permanent residence in the village, although a few middle-class people have built summer vacation homes in the hills. Our examination of birth places for married couples shows a marked preference for endogamy. And most of those born outside are from neighboring communes, and are consanguineally linked to persons in the village. The effect of small size, population stability, endogamy, alternative mating forms, and bilateral kinship is to relate most villagers to one another, and in a number of different ways. To the anthropologist this becomes clear when eliciting kin terms, for the villagers often have to decide which to invoke among several alternate routes of connection in arriving at a relationship. *"Tout le monde est parent,"* they say. ("We are all kinsmen.") In ordinary conversation, older relatives not lineally related to the speaker are called uncle and aunt, and kinsmen of the same age or younger than the speaker are called cousin.

The *quartiers,* where most interpersonal contacts among preschool children and among adults occur, tend to be kin units, since they are formed from the fragmentation of an original holding over several generations. The spatial arrangements of households frequently recapitulate their genealogical connections. In close proximity are the households of full and half siblings, who shared in the last division; they are surrounded by the homes of their first cousins, the children of parents' siblings who participated in a prior division; and so on.

Because they are composed of close kin, *quartiers* tend now to be exogamous. Within the *quartier,* therefore, persons are related through close consanguinity. Between *quartiers* they are related through affinity and more remote consanguinity. Kinship—beyond the household—does not generally provide a basis for corporation, but it does offer villagers lines of mutual access. This is especially true for women, since men also relate to each other through labor exchange or *coup-de-main* groups. Godparenthood reinforces actual kinship obligations where they are congruent, and extends obligations where genealogical ties are weak or nonexistent. Ritual kin ties are particularly apposite where wealth differences tend to obviate or overwhelm normal kin connections.

People who move into the village without kin ties are called outsiders and strangers, even though they have lived there many years and own land. The process of absorption takes more than one generation, and is accelerated when there are many children who marry within the commune.

Religion

A second source of integration is the common acceptance of the Roman Catholic Church. Everyone in Morne-Paysan is a Catholic. All infants are baptized in the church, and all children receive First Communion and are confirmed. All first marriages are celebrated by the priest. All persons hope to receive final rites at death. Most people exhibit the external insignia and behavior appropriate to their religion: they cross themselves when passing the church or a prominent shrine; they decorate their walls with religious pictures, particularly the Sacred Heart of Jesus; they light candles in the cemetery on All Saints' Eve. There are no adherents of either Protestant missionary sect: the Seventh Day Adventists and the Baptists. There are no adepts of the East Indian cult of Maldevidan. There are no Free Masons. And there are no members of the atheism-professing Martinique Communist party.

All this identification with the church notwithstanding, the priests protest bitterly about the lack of commitment and "true" faith among parishioners. They complain of inadequate financial support; poor church attendance and disrespect for the clergy, particularly from adult men; the persistence of "pagan" beliefs; and the high frequency of illegitimacy, consensual cohabitation, and adultery. These complaints are the usual themes of sermons. During Confirmation the village priest read a letter of welcome to the bishop, a list of grievances against the commune. He accused the villagers of a high rate of concubinage and conversely low rate of marriage (only two since the last episcopal visit). He railed against poor church attendance and contributions, saying that when they do come many just stand outside talking and smoking. He further complained about the attention given animals on Sunday morning in competition with the church. The bishop commented on all these, placing major blame on movies and magazines for the crisis in the Christian family. He advised people to subscribe to church periodicals and to support the parish. He used the example of the man who died at the cock pit and was denied church burial as an example of divine punishment. The confirmees were interrogated by the priests, who frequently had to prompt to elicit an acceptable response. One question muffed by all was the name of the sacrament required to start a Christian family.

It is clear that the degree of devotion varies considerably. Women tend to be more active in church affairs than men; and old people and children are more active than adolescents and younger adults. Old women, especially spinster schoolteachers, are most faithful. They attend mass each Sunday, as well as on many special occasions. They regularly go to confession and take communion. They form the core of the Legion of Mary, and of the religious sodalities which arrange funeral services for their members. These latter—*Bon Secours, Scapulaire,* and *Sacré Coeur*—in exchange for annual dues of 50 to 400 francs per year, entitle their members to requiem masses and to first-class funerals, in which the survivors accompany the casket from the church to the cemetery, holding banners and other emblems.

Younger women and most men of all ages rarely take communion. Many adult men do not recall the last time they went to confession; one man, over forty, thought he must have gone at least once since his confirmation, but was not sure. A number of women told us that they do not confess because they are unable or unwilling to discontinue behavior of which the priest disapproves. These include living *en ménage,* adultery, and attempts at contraception. Many men do not attend the Sunday morning service. They accompany their families to the *bourg,* and as the women and children enter the church, the men sit out the service in nearby bars. Most men prefer to stand than kneel at appropriate moments in the service, in order, they say, not to soil their trousers.

The attitudes of many villagers toward the clergy are ambivalent at best. In part this is because Martinique is still a missionary area, and there is not a sufficient number of native priests. The village priest is often alien, therefore, not only to the village but also to the island. Those who come from Ireland, Holland, Canada, and Flemish-speaking Belgium often have difficulties making themselves understood in French, and for quite a few years they are unable to speak or understand Creole.

Many men are openly critical of the priests. They frequently personalize their attitude toward the church in terms of their relationships with the local cleric, just as their identification with a particular political party is a question not of ideology but of their relationship with the party leader. There was a change of priests during our stay in the village; some people stopped attending services, while others began anew. The priest is quite isolated in the village and if he is to have any social life at all it is difficult for him not to become involved with one or another faction. One man stopped attending services because the priest rented his pew—which he had maintained for forty years and his father had before that—to someone else. Another complained of the priest's association with the mayor, the leader of party in power. A third said the priest, after not saying *bonjour* to him, accused him of being impolite; to which the man replied, "I don't need *you* to give me lessons in courtesy." Excepting the current priest, whom he "loves like a brother," one man dismissed them all as imbeciles. They resent the carping on their connubial statuses, and are particularly incensed by the Legion of Mary, whose members visit couples residing consensually in the hopes of getting them to "regularize" their relationships. Most people do marry eventually, as we have seen, which may partially account for the more active church participation of older villagers. Some villagers object to the fees they must pay for special masses and different classes of funerals.

Priests protest the tenacity of beliefs in supernatural beings derived from Africa and from a European folk stratum which fall outside orthodox Christianity. Some of these were mentioned in our discussion of health and curing: *zombis,* the resurrected dead manipulated nefariously; *engagés,* living persons who have contracted with the devil for power in return for their soul; *loups-garoux* or werewolves, who can shed their human form and assume that of animals, and so on. Specialists in dealing with these evil manifestations, both in their elicitation and exorcism, are known as *quimboiseurs.* There is no organized cult devoted to these beings in opposition or competition with the established church. While there are few who categorically assert such phenomena do not exist, the beliefs remain at the level of free-floating anxiety, and are not calls to action. The only "pagan" events which serve as points of large scale congregation are the wake within the village, a time of almost total assemblage despite the active opposition of the clergy; and the Carnival in Fort-de-France, or rather the funeral of Carnival on Ash Wednesday, when thousands of mourners, *guiablesses,* dressed in black and white, some bearing replicas of skulls, parade chanting through the streets of the capital. Although few adults of Morne-Paysan bother to go to Fort-de-France for Carnival, attendance at the *veillée* underscores both the integration of the village and the unwillingness of villagers to allow the church to restrict their activities.

No holiday, sacred or secular, passes without some recognition in the village. Flags are hung and speeches made on Bastille Day, the cemetery is illuminated on All Saints' Eve, there are dances during Carnival and around the New Year, and church services are well attended on Christmas and Easter. These days are shared, of course, with other villages and, indeed, with much of the world.

The greatest festivities are occasioned by the patron saint's day, and occur on two or three successive Sundays. Notices posted on walls announce the activities:

Saturday, 16 November

6 P.M.	Bell Ringing.	
	Fire Works.	

Sunday, 17 November

5 A.M.	Bell Ringing.	
9 A.M.	Assembly at the Town Hall. Parade to the Church.	
9:30 A.M.	Solemn Mass.	
	Wreath laid at Monument to the Dead of the World War.	
	Minute of Silence	
11 A.M.	Reception at the Town Hall. Distribution of cakes to the children.	
noon	Bell Ringing.	
3 P.M.	Bicycle Race.	Prizes: 3000 francs, 2000, 1000.
	Horse Race.	Prizes: 4000, 2500, 1500.
	Mule Race.	Prizes: 2500, 1500, 500.
	Jackass Race.	Prizes: 2000, 1000, 500.
6 P.M.	Bell Ringing.	
	Outdoor Movies.	
9 P.M.	Fire Works.	
	Public Ball in the Town Hall.	

Sunday, 24 November

11 A.M.	Competition and prizes awarded for the best exhibited fruits and vegetables of the commune.
3 P.M.	Foot races
	Adults. Prizes: 2000, 1500, 500.
	Adolescents. Prizes: 2000, 1500, 500.
	Children. Prizes: 500, 300, 200.
9 P.M.	Competition and prizes for *échoppes* [covered stall bars.]
	The Mayor invites his constituents to take part in the festivities, and to decorate their homes with bunting and lights. Liquor may be sold in *échoppes* and at dances during the festivities, in accordance with the law.

The festivities were limited to two Sundays, since some objected that the third would fall on Advent. During the week before the events, people were asked to subscribe to a donor's list. The only villagers who contributed—in amounts from 500 to 1500 francs—were those associated politically with the mayor. The contributions underwrote the expenses of the contest prizes and orchestra at the public dance. The *échoppes* were built in advance. They are made of a few bamboo posts supporting corrugated iron roofs. The sides are covered with banana and woven palm leaves, and the front left open. Interiors are elaborately hung with bedspreads, sheets, tablecloths, and bunting. Mirrors and secular pictures, like Millet's "Gleaners," are hung on the wall, and colored papers stream from the ceiling. Tables, chairs, and boxes holding bottles of rum, wine, beer, and soda are on the earthen floor. Those *échoppes* near the town hall are electrified by tapping the public current, and have electric lights and radios. Some of them have charcoal stoves, where women prepare creole foods. Most are set up by villagers who run bars and have liquor licenses. The effect, especially at night, is very colorful, loud, and animated.

The interior of a temporary bar or échoppe, *built for the annual patron saint's festivities.*

These *fêtes patronales* attract large numbers of professional gamblers, who travel from *fête* to *fête* with their gaming tables and accomplices. They set up their tables in the street around the church and in the sheltered outside corridors of the girls' school. The games are craps, various kinds of dice-determined racing, dominoes, card games, and three-card monte complete with shill, who "cheats" to win while the dealer absently turns his head away, and generally excites the crowd.

The games are most active at night, when each is illuminated by a single kerosene lamp. Children tend toward the racing tables, where the stakes are very low, while men play dice, cards, and dominoes. Women have nothing to do with gambling, neither managing nor playing. At night the gamblers sleep in the school courtyard, and at the close of festivities, pack up to go to another town. (Since there are thirty-four communes in Martinique, and some of the large *quartiers* also celebrate their saints' days, these men can be employed in gambling throughout the year.)

For the mayor the *fête* provides a forum for political speechmaking. Honored guests are prominent members of the mayor's party from other parts of the island. The ceremonies which were supposed to begin at 11 A.M. were postponed until the electricity, regularly cut off at that hour, could be restored. The mayor said that people in the countryside should be able to hear the speeches over loudspeakers. Wine was served and the orchestra played. An old man very solemnly danced, and a little girl, in creole costume, sat in the center of the floor holding flowers. At about 12:30 power was restored. Each speaker was introduced simply: "The microphone is passed to Monsieur X. . . ." The mayor's speech inventoried the contributions of his administration: roads, increased social services, dispensary, etc. He attacked the present metropolitan government in a thinly cloaked appeal for his own party. Subsequent speakers developed the same theme, eulogizing the mayor, and praying to the patron saint to keep him in office. No members of the opposition party were in evidence that morning.

Afternoon events drew many spectators and few contestants. Four boys entered the bicycle race: Jojo, Paul, and Gaby François and their close friend, Girard. The course runs the length of the bourg, and is strenuous, uphill almost all the way. The older brothers held back to let Gaby win. Girard, who did not finish, received a third of the first place prize from Gaby.

In the evening, activities center about the bars, gambling tables, and dances. The public dance at the town hall used the same orchestra that had played there during the day. Although it was free more people stood outside peering in through doors and windows than were inside dancing. The other dance, held in a regular bar, had an admission fee of 700 francs per couple, or rather, per man—girls enter free. This dance was more crowded, perhaps because the orchestra was clearly superior, again with many people looking in through the windows. On the second Sunday, both dances charged an admission fee; the orchestra which played at the *mairie* was originally paid 20,000 francs and given the right to hold dances on the two subsequent Sundays for their own account. Although some people waited the third Sunday the orchestra did not show up.

The *échoppes* were judged by the mayor's wife. The contest was won by the wife of a member of the municipal council.

A less elaborate acknowledgement of the patron saint of Quartier Petitfleuve began with festivities in 1956. It now has a school for five- and six-year-old children, and a chapel. Inviting outsiders to join in the recognition of its patron saint is a means of further establishing its identity, repeating, in miniature, the process whereby Morne-Paysan separated from Covin.

Economics

We have often alluded to the peasant's feeling for his land, his pride in being independent of the estates. Sidney Mintz (1964*a*:xiv) states this independence simply:

> The history of newly discovered and newly occupied areas has demonstrated again and again that free men will not work as employed agricultural laborers if they have access to land which they can cultivate for themselves.

Morne-Paysan is a peasant village, in contrast and opposition to the estate orientation of most of Martinique. The only invited guest at the *fête patronale* who was not an official of the mayor's party, was in fact a political enemy: the socialist mayor of Morne Médaille. But he was invited because his village too emphasized vegetable and fruit cultivation, and the two communes occasionally unite on economic matters in the General Council.

The needs of small farmers and the needs of the plantations appeal to different politics. The small farmers are interested in local markets, agricultural diversification, and small-scale credit. The great planters are interested in overseas markets, monoculture, protective quotas, and large-scale credit. They are intimately associated with the import-export trade, and particularly with the transoceanic shipping firms who carry away their bananas, sugar, pineapples, and rum, and bring in manufactured items and metropolitan foodstuffs. National governments favor the large planters in part because the planters have the means of influencing legislation in their favor, whereas the peasants, particularly those in the former colonies, are most remote from political decision-making. The national government also profits from the large-scale taxes—customs duties—collected on shipments between the metropole and its overseas departments.

Martinique has always imported the bulk of its food. Even during the Vichy period, when overseas trade virtually ceased, plantation lands were not effectively put into food production, and the islanders depended upon peasant cultivation and doles from the United States. Officially it has been argued that self-sufficiency is desirable. "Since the eighteenth century, the Administration has constantly sanctioned a policy of agricultural diversification, oriented principally to food crops" (Préfecture de la Martinique 1964:48). In fact the tendency has been in the opposite direction. The amount of land in peasant production continues to decline, and the returns from the internal market are now threatened with the importations of new foods which are sold at the same or lower prices than those raised domestically. This appears to be due to more efficient European methods of production and to transportation subsidies, providing return cargoes for the banana and sugar boats. Both the planters and the agricultural proletarians make use of formal associations —trade associations and trade unions—to influence the economy in their direction. Since departmentalization the great planters have found few rewards in the electoral process, because most politicians represent the Communist or Socialist parties, but they continue to have access to the more powerful Paris-appointed prefecture, who is frequently sympathetic to their point of view.

Village peasants make only limited use of formal, secular organizations. A few years after the achievement of communal status, the mayor and some of his followers formed a mutual-aid society, called "The Future of Morne-Paysan." For an initiation fee of about 40 cents, and monthly dues of about 15 cents, a member receives small sums at times of births, sickness, and death, to supplement social security. But they have no lobby to influence legislation and no organization to provide general assistance for agricultural activities. In the last few years small loans at low interest rates have been made available for land acquisition and amelioration and housebuilding, and some of the villagers have joined a cooperative for the collective marketing of their crops. They are seeking not to bypass the market in general, but to sell directly to large consumers, such as schools and hospitals.

The mayor also organized a banana cooperative for wrapping the stems in protective envelopes, weighing them, and transporting them from the village to the pier. Since the average farmer, with less than a hundred trees, has little means for delivering his fruit to the docks, those persons who were politically opposed to the mayor were excluded from the market. Then a leader of the opposition founded a competitive cooperative with the aid of other prominent members of the Socialist party. He attempted to entice participants away from the mayor by offering a higher percentage of the selling price immediately. A few went over, but most, either through loyalty or fear of antagonizing the mayor, remained with the original cooperative. The opposition was unable to compete successfully and discontinued operations.

We have already mentioned the cooperative exchange groups, or *coup-de-mains,* which enable farmers periodically to tap larger labor resources than those provided by their own households. These groups are instances of the general ethic of hospitality and reciprocity, which pervades social interaction. In its simplest form it is reciprocal gift-giving, without any measure of relative values. When the *échoppes* were dismantled after the *fête patronale,* one woman spent the day returning tablecloths and bedspreads loaned to decorate her bar. At each house she left some tangerines. The resolution of petty quarrels may also involve exchange of small gifts, like fruit and flowers. *Coups-de-mains* serve to unite villagers not only because of the cooperative nature of the work, but also because they typically involve a physical displacement of persons who walk from their *quartiers* to some central point, and then disburse to reassemble another day at some other place. On *coup-de-main* they work, eat, and drink together, each in turn assuming the role of director and provender, at least of drink. Work for the *commune* itself may also take the form of a *coup-de-main,* when the budget provides no funds for labor. These serve less to integrate the village, however, than to throw into relief its division, for only those in political sympathy with the mayor turn out for such work. Labor contributed to the village constructed the town hall, and rebuilt homes which were demolished for road work. Departmental funds are provided for road work itself, and gangs are hired.

Politics

For a decade following the end of the Second World War the Martiniquan Communist party received a majority of the votes, and two of the three deputies representing the new department in Paris were communists. The Socialist party received most of the other votes, and almost every commune had either a Communist or a Socialist mayor. In 1956, the leader of the Communist party and deputy and mayor of Fort-de-France, Aimé Césaire, resigned to form his own Martiniquan Progressive party. Césaire, one of France's most celebrated poets, eloquently explains his resignation in a now-famous "Letter to Maurice Thorez" (1956). Accusing the French communists of a kind of imperialism, Césaire's hope was to form an Antillean-based movement, which would align itself with the African delegations in the French parliament. He did not anticipate the forthcoming independence of the francophone nations of Africa, which left him politically isolated in Paris. His party, which drew support from many former communists like himself and from a number of socialists, began to agitate for autonomy and away from increasing departmentalization which he had previously advocated.

The other political parties—the left-wing Unified Socialists, the Catholic centrists, and the conservative Regrouping of the French People (RPF) or Social Republicans—drew very little support. Only in Morne-Paysan and the fishing village of Grand'Rivière is there any RPF strength.

Except for Césaire's Progressive party, each of the Martiniquan political movements is organically associated with its metropolitan counterpart. The characteristic ideology of the party is voiced in the press, for each group in Martinique publishes a newspaper which the members are expected to buy and read. Some of these publications are shortlived, as party structures change frequently, and groups divide and recombine, but many appear for years. At party meetings and congresses, professionals from Europe are often present, and attempt to guarantee the political orthodoxy of the faithful.

Despite this tremendous emphasis on ideology, local political affiliations have much more to do with personal relationships between an individual and the local leadership. This is clearly the case in Morne-Paysan. While the general attitude toward politicians is negative—"politicians are thieves"—most men are identified with either the Socialists or the Gaullist RPF. But within the village, these labels are not descriptive of ideological differences. Indeed, the political situation at first was very confusing, because it seemed that the conservative RPF drew its supporters from the smallest landholders and landless villagers, while the Socialists included most of the larger landholders and the owner of the largest store. In addition there were ideological subgroupings which cut across the two parties. Some socialists and some Gaullists were stout Pétainists, associated with a "Movement for the Defense of the Memory of Marshall Pétain." These men held that far from being a traitor, Pétain enabled France to maintain some slight degree of autonomy during the Nazi period, and his patriotism is unquestionable. Others, from both parties, saw De Gaulle as the sole saviour of France, and opposed what they felt was an historical whitewash.

The basis for political factionalism became clear as we reconstructed the genealogies of the opponents. What appears as political opposition is familial and economic in origin, a split which has assumed a political expression relatively independent of ideological commitment.

During the years when Morne-Paysan formed a hamlet of Covin, recruitment to its few formal leadership positions—such as supervisor of the civil registry and member of the Covin municipal council—was from a group of large landowners, the light-skinned, frequently illegitimate, descendants and their affines of those whites who were the great planters during the middle of the nineteenth century. Through bequests to their legal offspring and false acts of sale to their natural children the holdings were transferred, and their grandchildren and greatgrandchildren today are large farmers, the school directors and teachers, and the owner of the biggest and most modern store.

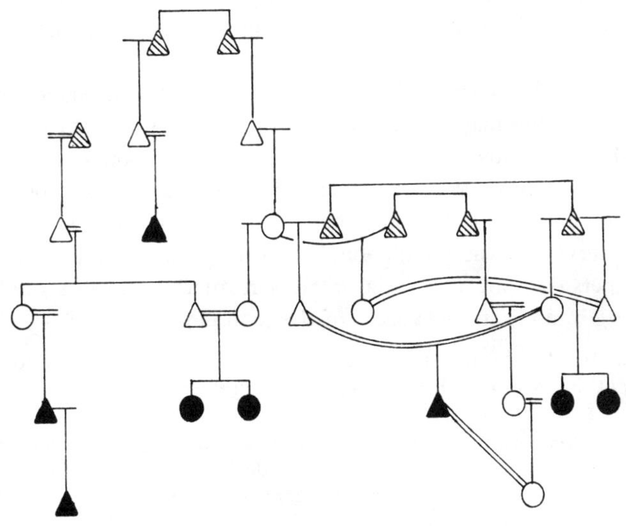

PARTIAL GENEALOGY OF SOCIALIST LEADERS

When the commune was established municipal elections were held, following the metropolitan laws of April 5, 1884. These people, as Socialists, formed a list and won. A schoolteacher, Mlle. de la Roche, was elected mayor.

The opposition, led by Monsieur Dubin, himself an outsider who had recently purchased a very large farm in the village, protested the results, claiming a fraudulent ballot count. The prefecture acceded to the protest and scheduled a second election. Local political campaigns in Martinique have the reputation of being rough, and this was no exception. There were claims and counterclaims of miscount, and both sides accused the other of having imported toughs to intimidate voters and steal the ballot boxes. When the campaign was over the opposition, with Dubin as mayor, was installed and has not subsequently been unseated. Dubin was later also elected to represent the village in the General Council, the departmental legislature.

Dubin, as a Gaullist, received the core of his strength from his tenants, the members of three or four very large family groups, dark-skinned descendants of ex-slaves who received no property from the early landowners. He capitalized on the resentment of the landless toward the landowners, but had to be a landowner himself to create ties of dependency between him and his supporters. Most of his land is divided into small tracts, cultivated on shares. All his tenants support him in public, attend his receptions, accompany him to the capital for political demonstrations. They recognize that the balance of benefits of this relationship is weighted toward the mayor, but being landless they have little alternative. One of his tenants complained bitterly in private about the low price paid by the mayor's banana cooperative. When it was suggested that it was partially his own fault since he said nothing to the mayor, he sarcastically replied that it was also his own fault that he had no land.

The main political reward is the distribution of local patronage, especially road work. In principle the mayor's authority is limited by the municipal council, fifteen villagers who are elected with him; in fact they are almost never consulted. Several councillors privately resented their being bypassed, but none protested publicly or to the mayor himself. They noted that the communal jeep, which was supposed to be at the service of the population, was usually unavailable because it became the mayor's personal car. The socialist press regularly publishes implications of Dubin's enriching himself at the expense of the commune or state:

> Dubin believes there are no restrictions on his actions, and claims to all who listen: "I do nothing without the counsel of the Prefecture." . . .
>
> At totally non-competitive prices, Dubin awarded a transport contract to the owner of truck no. 46–PL–6854. The payments are made in the name of the driver, who in fact receives only 500 francs a day. The real owner is Dubin! Is this not misappropriation?

The mayor uses his position to distribute paid communal work among his supporters, and to facilitate their receiving social security and medical benefits. As a stranger with no resident kinsmen he has had to develop other ties to the villagers, and frequently serves as a godfather. Every few days he makes a circuit of bars, chatting and buying drinks. He is a skilled spontaneous speechmaker, and though relatively uneducated and often grammatically imprecise—a point noted frequently within the village—he is a skilled rhetorician. At funerals, on patron saint's days, on Bastille Day, and at other times he seizes the occasion to address the crowd, stressing his identification with de Gaulle and the Free French Forces. (Actually he remained in Martinique during the Occupation, although a number of villagers fled by fishing boat to Dominica, where they made contact with de Gaulle's agents.) On one occasion Dubin organized his followers for an anticommunist counterdemonstration in Fort-de-France. They received word from the prefecture that all demonstrations were prohibited, and that rural people were not to assemble in the city. The mayor explained that they were obligated not to be the first to violate the prefect's command, but to be prepared to demonstrate if the communists did. He reviewed the history of recent events in Algeria. Short, thin, consumptive looking, waving his arms in the air, he began to rock on his heels. "We are men of order. But if it becomes a question of disorder, we shall create disorder!" Occasional mild applause, and a few cries of "Vive de Gaulle" punctuated his speech. As soon as he finished a man stood up and, misinterpreting everything the mayor said, agreed with him and pledged to him the loyalty of the villagers.

The Socialists have a monopoly of higher education in Morne-Paysan. All the schoolteachers are members of the party, as are most of the Lycée graduates. The director of the boy's school is the closest to being a learned man in the village. Every evening men gather at his house to talk about politics and agriculture, and play dominoes. Several times during the evening one of his children passes a tray with rum, beer, and soda. The director is tall, handsome, of unmixed European ancestry. His wife is colored. His children, both of legitimate and adulterous birth, live with him. He is a teacher, with excellent command of French, but he is just as willing to speak Creole. Anyone appears to be welcome in his house, and he is always kind and solicitous to the poor cultivators who attend without contributing to the discussions. Although he does not approve of the mayor, he never initiates attacks on him. His guests are under no such restrictions; the mayor is a frequent butt of sarcasm and angry denunciation.

As the mayor consolidated his strength following the failure of his opponents' banana cooperative, the Socialists withdrew from active opposition. With no expectation of victory they gave only token performances in recent campaigns. Having effectively renounced political ambitions, however, they no longer had to maintain a high level of transactions with their former followers, in the exchange of land through tenancy for votes. Several of them opted to remove land from tenancy and put it into pasturage. Instead of letting the land in many small tracts whose *colons* and their families were expected to support the owners politically, they have aggregated lands, terminated tenancy, and hired a few day laborers to care for the cattle. Since milk and beef give greater returns than vegetables distributed in the internal market system, the owners have decided to maximize economic gains at the expense of possible political opportunities.

Courts

The judicial organization of the metropole obtains in Martinique: people have access to several levels of tribunal, culminating in a court of appeals. Law is an active profession, and a school of jurisprudence is the only university branch on the island. The municipalities are vested with certain legal functions, particularly those relating to the registration of births, legitimations and recognitions, marriages, and deaths. All marriages require a civil ceremony, and the mayor is empowered to act for the state. Police, especially the quasi-military gendarmes, have certain judicial functions; they not only enforce laws of traffic, for example, but assess and collect fines for contraventions. Inheritances are recorded by a notary and registered with the state, and those which involve land may require an official survey.

Rural people are aware of these courts, and many have a good idea of how they operate. Yet there is a general reluctance to use them, an unwillingness to take disputes out of the village where if they cannot be resolved they may at least be controlled. For example, unmarried mothers know—or if they don't the nurse tells them—that they may force support from their children's fathers for a certain period of time, and occasionally a woman threatens to initiate a paternity claim. But no one has actually gone through with it. They say, *"mwê pa le fe zistwa,"* "I don't want to start stories," (that is, troubles). There is almost as much reluctance to make a formal complaint as there is fear of having to defend oneself.

There are two situations in which recourse to the courts, while not common, is occasionally sought. The first is disputes about inheritance when some of the heirs no longer live in the village. There are times when a formal land distribution is not made upon the death of its owner, and the land is kept undivided for a generation or more. As long as the heirs are in close contact they are able to agree on sharing the produce. As some heirs or the children move off, or die, it becomes increasingly difficult to maintain the original agreements. Those heirs who have left and intend never to return to the village may attempt to force a division in court, in order to be able to sell off their share. This is tedious and expensive, especially if more than a generation has elapsed, because it is not easy to track down and gain the accord of all legal participants. Where there is any expectation of returning to the village, attempts are made to resolve the distribution among the disputants. One woman claims that she would like to force a distribution in court, but she is unwilling alone to assume all the legal expenses.

The other source of disputes whose resolution is sometimes sought in the courts is found in the relationship between shopkeepers and clients. There are a half-dozen stores in the village, selling essential items which are not locally produced. The smaller ones stock only a limited selection of canned goods, flour, oil, matches, cigarettes, kerosene, salt, sugar, and rum. The larger ones have more groceries, and offer hardware, kitchen utensils, seed, drygoods, and school supplies. There is no bargaining in the stores and bread, the main staple, is sold at a government-fixed price.

Although several stores and bars have signs which deny it, all shopkeepers do most of their business on credit, for customers have cash only during certain times of the year. Each regular customer has a notebook in which the amount of her purchases is recorded, and the shopkeeper also maintains a record. A typical daily menu for a poor although not impoverished household of two adults and four children shows how quickly a sizeable bill can be accumulated:

Morning:

bread, 1 kilogram	60 francs
margarine	50
milk, 1 liter (not purchased at store)	60
coffee or cacao	25

Noon:	
oil, 250 grams	60
dried fish, 500 grams	160
lentils or peas, 250 grams	120
Evening:	
vegetable soup (if not home grown)	100
bread, 1 kilogram	60
pudding with leftover milk	
kerosene, 1 liter	25

Many accounts await settlement until the quarterly receipt of family allocations.

The relationship between buyer and seller is often tense and potentially fragile yet both parties have a vested interest in maintaining it. The shopkeeper extends credit to establish the relationship, and must not be too demanding or he loses that customer and possibly others who seek a more compliant patron. The customer must pay eventually, or be denied credit by all stores. If he refuses to make some payment, or delays overlong, he risks being called to court. The economist Polanyi noted the general interpersonal antagonism which accompanies profit-making transactions relating to food. "No community intent on protecting the fount of solidarity between its members can allow latent hostility to develop around a matter as vital to animal existence and, therefore, capable of arousing as tense anxieties as food" (1957:255). In December 1957, a shopkeeper in Quartier Petitfleuve took three of his customers to court to force payment of debts which had accumulated during two years. The three were condemned and ordered to pay. Court costs were added, more than tripling the amount owed. Since the court now has its own claim against the defendants, they are threatened with seizure of their possessions. One of the three felt that he was being made to pay the costs of all, since he owned some land and a carpenter's workshop, while the others had no property.

Villagers recognize that store accounts should be paid, but they feel that the shopkeepers press too hard for their money and their prices are too high. The hostility toward them is sometimes manifest in accusations of witchcraft. In fact, one shopkeeper admitted that she employs a peripatetic *quimboiseur* to stimulate business at her shop and attract customers away from others. The magician is a Guadeloupian who visits Martinique twice a year, and seems to have a rather extensive clientele. He received 50,000 francs and a gold ring in exchange for a silver amulet and certain verbal charms.

The most serious accusation is made against Monsieur Brun, the owner of the largest store. Since Brun is a leader of the opposition, the mayor has given it his credence, and encourages his followers to repeat the story to each other and to outsiders. A few years before we came to the village a three year old child disappeared. At 1 P.M. he had been playing in front of the church. Thirty minutes later he was gone. Although the police investigated, officially the case is unsolved; they determined neither what happened nor whether the child is still alive. The event terrified the villagers, for it seemed necessarily to implicate one or more of their neighbors and kinsmen. The following story circulated:

> Brun saw the child playing near his store. When he saw he was alone, he enticed him into the store with candy. In the house with him was his father's brother,

Frederic, and his father's daughter, Marie. Brun whipped up some kind of potion and told the child to drink. The child tasted it and refused to drink any more. Brun told him if he drank it he would give him more candy. The child finished the draught and fell inert. Marie had been told in the meantime to leave the room. By devious route the sleeping child was spirited to Brun's father's farm, and the two of them pierced his throat, cut him open, and removed the intestines. Then they sawed him in three pieces, and carried the remains to a sorcerer in Fort-de-France. Brun and his father are *engagés* of the devil, and their contract requires supplying their mentor with a human soul in order not to forfeit their own. In order to stop Marie from talking, Brun tried to poison her. He was unsuccessful, but in the process five dogs died. Brun successfully poisoned his uncle.

9

Some Other Caribbean Villages

IN THE FIRST CHAPTER, I outlined the major characteristics of the West Indian culture area: a common history of plantation agriculture for export, Negro slavery, and political colonialism. We saw that despite these shared traits there are important differences among the islands, and even between plantation and peasant regions on the same island. From there we turned to an ethnographic description and analysis of one village on one island. This chapter returns to the larger perspective, to place Morne-Paysan in the context of rural villages from other parts of the Caribbean and to give some appreciation of the range of variation in the area. I have chosen for brief comparison peasant and plantation villages on Jamaica, Puerto Rico, and in British Guiana, on the South American mainland.

Guianese Villages

AUGUST TOWN Raymond T. Smith described three villages in British Guiana in his classic study of the Negro family (1956). Like Morne-Paysan they are essentially postemancipation settlements. Two of them, August Town and Better Hope, were purchased by freed slaves, while the third, Perseverance, was settled by squatters who later acquired legal title. There appears to have been a continuity of personnel, for those who bought the estates were its former slave laborers. One can imagine the emotional feeling of the freed men of August Town who wrote: " . . . we the undersigned proprietors of plantation No. 21 called Saint Pauls on this tenth day of July 1865 hereby enter into mutual agreement . . ." In Martinique there was never any possibility of obtaining estate lands; emancipation meant either quitting the plantations for the peasant life in the hills, or remaining as wage laborers.

August Town is today divided into three parallel sections, running about 9 miles from the sea to a river. Between two of the sections, corresponding to separately purchased parts of the original estates, and the third, there is a private estate owned by a man of East Indian ancestry. Drainage ditches providing irrigation for the rice fields and some degree of flood control border the sections and the estate.

Settlement is concentrated narrowly on either side of a road near the sea wall. The church and school are in one section and the stores are strung out along the road. Many of the houses in the dwelling area have small gardens on which some produce is grown, but most agricultural land stretches out from the residential area to the river, and no houses are built on it.

Household gardens, provision lands and rice lands are held in fee simple, while pasturage is leased from the Crown by groups of villages and used collectively. Productive fields are extremely small, and most of the crop is consumed at home, with some sale in the village. Household groups exploit provision lands, while rice fields require larger groups, especially for the harvest. There are no cooperative labor exchange groups:

> There is very little development of a system of reciprocal kinship obligations, and although ties of kinship or friendship may be invoked as the basis for reciprocal help, the main mechanism operates through the medium of monetary exchange. . . . In August Town, cash payment for rice cutting is the rule even between members of the same household group (Smith:31).

The households are not corporate, for they neither own nor exploit collectively. Income is derived primarily from outside employment on the sugar estates and in the bauxite fields, rather than from their own lands. Almost all men from about eighteen years and older leave the village for employment elsewhere.

Outside marketing is of little significance and does not provide an economic role for the household women. The majority of conjugal unions in August Town and Perseverance, however, despite the necessity of finding wage labor outside on estates and mines, are endogamous. In Better Hope, which is more extensively differentiated internally, more than 65 percent of the unions count one or both partners from the outside. According to Smith, endogamy provides a greater feeling of security. "If they enter a union with someone from another part of the colony they will perforce have to form new and difficult relationships with strange persons, an experience which can be avoided by marrying someone whose family and background they know already" (Smith:187).

Smith feels that the family types he isolated cannot be explained in terms of the local village but require the context of the larger society. The village is not a self-contained system. The villagers do assert a unity and a common purpose. As in Morne-Paysan they say that August Town is a "black people's village," in which they are "all one family." The claimed solidarity is seen not in politics or religion, but at the wake, where each household is supposed to be represented.

Smith finds four groups significantly differentiated to form a system of stratification within the village. The criteria of differentiation are relevant to the society as a whole, rather than merely to the village itself. The groups form a three-tiered hierarchy (Smith:211):

Elite Group

"White Collar" occupations
Ethnically diverse
Culturally distinct
Mostly "strangers" to the village
Approximately twenty persons.

School-Teacher Clique
Mainly Negro
Culturally intermediate, but tending towards that of elite group
Kinship ties in the village
Approximately ten persons.

Business Group
Mainly non-Negro
Culturally belonging to the main village group
Approximately thirty persons.

Main Village Group
"Black people"
"All one family"
Approximately 1700 persons.

This scheme is for August Town. Perseverance is somewhat more homogeneous, and Better Hope somewhat less.

This account of a highly detailed study does it little justice. The important point is that land ownership correlates with a certain development of village organization and identification, expressed through verbal sentiments, endogamy, and assemblage at wakes. The integration attained is limited by the necessity of finding outside employment, since farms are inadequate sources of income. The village does not contain corporate subunits, such as households or labor groups. Labor as a commodity is a much more developed notion than in the Martinique highlands. Even the extension of kinship in August Town provides only a limited network of relationships, although it does restrict the development of status differentiation.

CANALVILLE Elliott P. Skinner (1955) is interested in interaction among ethnic groups in British Guiana and selected a village ethnically more differentiated than August Town. Canalville includes persons of African and East Indian ancestry, as well as a few Chinese and Portuguese. Although there are differences in religion, marriage customs, and food habits between the Africans and East Indians, Skinner feels that cultural opposition is expressed primarily in terms of the stereotypes each group has of the other; the Negroes claim that the East Indians are tightwads, the East Indians that the Negroes are spendthrifts. Friendly interaction does occur between members of the two groups. A Negro, angry with an East Indian, cursed him saying, "You good-for-nothing coolie." Then he suddenly saw an East Indian friend, and stopped, explaining, "Me can't talk over much, cause this boy here is me neighbor and it go hurt he."

Many men work on a nearby sugar plantation, but all prefer to work their own lands independent of the estate. In contrast to August Town, very few men leave the village for work in the mines. Holdings range from 1 to 10 acres. As in Morne-Paysan, women, either wives or female relatives of the farmers, take the produce for sale in the city, for there is no market in the village.

> Canalville is primarily a small-scale farming community in which most families farm either for commercial purposes or for home and family consumption. Many villagers are engaged in nonfarming occupations, but a man does not feel "independent" if he does not have crops growing. This has been true of the villagers since the community came into existence 100 years ago (Skinner:103).

Like August Town, Canalville is threatened periodically with flooding from the sea, and successful settlement requires elaborate drainage and irrigation systems under village control. Houses stretch out along the main road parallel to the Demerara River, with farm lands marked off in regular rectangles in the back dam. Each plot is separated from the next by drainage ditches.

Religion is divisive rather than integrative. The Negroes are members of various Christian sects, and the East Indians are divided between Hindus and Moslems. Nonetheless, funerals call for total assemblage independent of the religious affiliation of the deceased. Labor-exchange groups, called "being friendly," and "boxes" also unite persons across ethnic boundaries.

> A "box" is an organized group in which each member gives a certain amount of money, about a dollar, to the "keeper" of the box, and the keeper gives one member all the money he has collected. This money is called a "hand" and every week a different member of the box receives a hand until all the members have been paid (Skinner:128).

There are tensions in the village which counter the integration encouraged by peasant proprietorship. People steal from each other's lands, and each plot is prominently marked with a "No Trespassing" sign. An apprehended thief is delivered to the police for judicial action. This is in marked contrast to Morne-Paysan, where most people would elect to suffer the loss rather than appeal to the courts. The tensions in Canalville seem related not only to ethnic heterogeneity and the necessity of finding work on the estates, but also a regular turnover in population. Most of the present inhabitants are not descendants of the original freeholders; ". . . there has been a steady exchange of population between Canalville and the rest of the colony" (Skinner:94). Such mobility lessens the expectations of mutual obligation which emerge among a stable population.

The Puerto Rican Municipio

Under the direction of Julian H. Steward, a team of anthropologists from Columbia University carried out field research in Puerto Rico in 1948 and 1949. They selected four areas for intensive study, each emphasizing a different agricultural system: tobacco and mixed crops; coffee; sugarcane on a government-owned estate; and sugarcane on a privately owned estate. We shall consider here the first and last types. Puerto Rico, Cuba, and Santo Domingo differ from other Caribbean areas in their relatively low percentages of persons of African descent. Slavery came late to these islands, although it endured after emancipation in the British and French colonies, and the majority of the people are considered to be of European descent, both culturally and racially.

TABARA The *municipio* Tabara, studied by Robert A. Manners, has a population of more than 17,000, many times larger than Morne-Paysan or the Guianese villages. Manners focused his analysis on Quito, one of seven constituent *barrios* of Tabara, and within Quito he concentrated on a particular neighborhood or *poblado* (which corresponds to the Martiniquan *quartier*). Tabara was never a region of intensive slavery. In 1828, forty-five years before emancipation, there were only 395 slaves in a population of 3453 persons. Of the freemen, 2558 were classified as white, 339 mulatto, 83 Negro, and 78 squatters for whom color was not specified.

The settlement pattern was introduced from Spain, and turns up again and again in Latin America. The *municipio* is divided into two types of section: the central town or *pueblo,* with a church and plaza, near which are the agencies of government; and the outlying *barrios* of farm lands and rural dwellers. Residence is stratified by class in the nucleated *pueblo,* where the houses sit neatly along regular streets. In the *barrios* there is much less status differentiation, and housing tends to be dispersed. These *barrios* are to a degree self-sufficient. "Apart from the need for the church, the medical services and other pueblo-provided services, the local neighborhood supplies most of the daily needs of its residents" (Manners 1956:103).

Tobacco is cultivated under a system of sharecropping called *a medias* (similar to *moitié-moitié* in Morne-Paysan). The owner and tenant share the costs of production and split the proceeds from the sale. Foodstuffs are cultivated with hired laborers. There is no cash tenancy. Cooperative labor exchange used to be common, but is today very rare. The groups, called *junta de ayuda,* were used in rice fields. The term referred both to the system of a group of men working for a single farmer in exchange for a specified portion of the crop and to a group of small farmers who combined to work each other's land. The development of tobacco cultivation for cash, which permitted a shift away from subsistence horticulture, "hastened the disappearance of rice production and with it the *ayuda*" (Manners:114).

Land tenure in Tabara is much much fluid than in Morne-Paysan or in the Guianese villages, for land is acquired principally by purchase, not by inheritance. Land is rarely held in the same family for three or even two generations. There is a continual movement to and from the area as new persons, perhaps after a successful year of sharecropping, find the means to purchase land.

Although both tobacco and food are grown for sale, the latter in urban markets, the farmer's wife is not involved in the market. Tobacco is sold directly through a growers' cooperative, and fruits and vegetables are sold to local truckers who resell in Rio Piedras and other cities. These *negociantes* meet the farmers at specified places, usually at rural stores along the roads, to discuss prices. Occasionally a trucker has an arrangement with a farmer whereby he sells for him and retains an agreed percentage for his services. The great proliferation of retail shops in the municipality—there are more than 200 of them—means that the farmers need not travel to the city to obtain supplies. As elsewhere in the Caribbean, these shops do much of their business on credit.

Tabara is highly stratified on economic grounds. Manners found three classes in both the pueblo and the barrio; each class is itself internally stratified, with reference not only to wealth but also to rural-urban association. He charts these groups as follows, the letters "R" and "U" referring to "rural" and "urban" (Manners:136):

TABLE 17

OCCUPATIONAL-ECONOMIC CLASSES OF TABARA

Urban	Rural
I. Upper	
A. Large Merchants (RU)	Summer Residents (R)
Doctors (U)	Landholders of over 100 *Cuerdas* (RU)
Top Government Employees (U)	
B. Professionals (RU)	Landholders of 35–100 *Cuerdas* (RU)
Medium Merchants (RU)	
II. Middle	
Truckers (*Negociantes*) (RU)	Landholders of 8–35 *Cuerdas* (R)
Small Storekeepers (RU)	
Veterans (RU)	
Chauffeurs (RU)	
III. Lower	
Vendors (U)	Landholders of 1–8 *Cuerdas* (R)
Artisans (RU)	Sharecroppers (*Medianeros*) (R)
Day Laborers (U)	Squatters (*Agregados*) (R)

The classes stand in relations of deference and respect to each other. The upper classes enjoy privileges denied the lower. They maintain a social club which excludes persons of low income and those of demonstrable Negro ancestry. A young people's affiliate formally excludes men who "dance with servants in 'bad places'." Wealthy girls no longer join the Daughters of Mary, because it has become identified with girls of poorer families. Children playing baseball usually "have a ball-chaser in the person of one of the children of an agricultural laborer" (Manners:135).

Much of the interclass tension typically associated with stratified agrarian societies is mitigated here because of the very real possibility of social mobility. Sharecroppers regularly enter the landowning class, because tobacco does not require the capital investment in land, labor, and machinery necessary for the exploitation of sugar and coffee. Frugality is valued, especially among the lower classes, and in contrast to much of Puerto Rico, they rarely gamble. Tobacco farmers suffer a dead time of only three months a year, compared with the six or more month dead period in sugar. Potential mobility, according to Manners, has weakened the system of godparenthood which is so strong in the sugar areas, for the mutual obligations among *compadres* are based largely upon status equality of long duration. Relations between a new landholder and his tenant conflict with those of *compadrazgo.*

Where landowners are resident and in direct management, paternalism governs their relations to their tenants. "Face-to-face relationships between landlord and tenant remain strong in the tobacco-minor crops region despite the decline in intensity of many of the respect patterns of the old *patrón-agregado* days" (Manners:165). Local officials seek to maintain office by dispensing patronage, primarily in selecting laborers for government-supported road projects.

The degree of integration achieved in Tabara is much less and of a different kind from that in Morne-Paysan. In the latter village, widespread control of land and the stability and basic homogeneity of the population is crucial in the kind of structure which developed. The subcultural variations which Manners associates with class, and the involvement of the elite in an island-wide network of communication and association do not facilitate any notion that the people of Tabara are "all one family." On the other hand, while heterogeneous and class-structured, Tabara does not attain the rigidity of stratification found in sugar towns. Identification here is with class rather than community, but the possibility of mobility and the presence of a middle class precludes the clear opposition of class on the estates.

CAÑAMELAR Cañamelar, studied by Sidney W. Mintz, is a *municipio* in an area dominated by an absentee sugar corporation which controls access to all employment in the region. The southern coast of Puerto Rico had long been planted in cane, but until the American occupation of 1899 plantations were family-run *haciendas,* characterized in principle by stable paternalistic relationships between the owner and his workers. In Cañamelar the *haciendas* were sold to a mainland-based corporation which had the capital to amalgamate vast holdings and establish highly efficient factories. In the classification of Wagley and Harris (1955:433–435), the plantation changed from an *engenho* to a *usina.* This is the customary organization of the plantation in most of the West Indies, particularly Cuba, Barbados, Jamaica, and Guadeloupe, although not of Martinique, in which most estates remain in resident family control.

Cañamelar is a town and seven *barrios.* Most people live rent free on estate lands in compact clusters of houses called *colonias* and on the public domain along the roads and beaches. Mintz feels that the strategic unit of study is not the *municipio* nor even the *barrio,* but one "tract of corporate cane land, with all the local forces—men, machines, and managerial staff—required to operate it profitably" (1966:326). In the center is a plaza which was once the courtyard of the *hacienda.* Local managerial representatives live around the plaza: the head overseer (*mayordomo primero*), the head of the company store, the assistant overseers, and the bookkeepers. The warehouse, store, and office are also near the plaza. Nearby are two barrack-like structures of 10 two-room apartments each, a more recently constructed settlement of 38 two-room houses with outside kitchens, and some smaller groups of houses. Although the company-owned houses are superior in construction to those built by workers on government land, people prefer the beach to the *colonia.* Those on company lands are called *agregado;* those on government land are called *independizado.*

In every agricultural region there are seasonal changes which affect the tempo of work, alternating periods of intense and limited activity. In Cañamelar there are two seasons: the harvest (*zafia*) during which there is work, and the dead time (*tiempo muerto*) during which there is none. Each lasts about half the year. A strong cycle of euphoria and dysphoria is correlated with these seasons. Mintz says that if the harvest has begun by Christmas the holiday is celebrated with gaiety and festivity; if the harvest is delayed, Christmas is an unfestive occasion of reserved participation. Once the harvest begins people buy more food and luxury items, beer, clothing, and furniture. "Long deferred baptismal ceremonies are held and godparents fulfill their traditional obligations, thus creating new bonds at a time when the participants can best afford it" (Mintz:352–353).

During the harvest there is work not only for residents but also for outsiders. The estate managers encourage migration from the highlands, for these workers are not unionized and are willing to accept piece work and incentive rates. While these give higher wages, they also shorten the season to the benefit of the migrants and the managers and the detriment of the regular workers. The hostility between the two groups of laborers is intensified by the lack of ritual, affinal, and consanguineal ties among them.

Mintz charts the stratification of Cañamelar as follows (Mintz:392):

TABLE 18

SOCIAL ORGANIZATION OF CAÑAMELAR MUNICIPALITY

Urban	Rural
Absentee landowners Quasi-absentees: house *rentiers*, theater owner, pharmacy owner Local: *colono*	
PROFESSIONALS AND OFFICALS	
School superintendent, visiting doctor and dentists, minister and family (teachers and engineer), pharmacists, water works engineer, the most important teachers.	Hacienda administrators and *mayordomos* on biggest *colonias*.
OFFICEHOLDERS, RETAILERS, SUPPLIERS OF SERVICE	
Mayor, auditor, treasurer, internal revenue agent and assistant, tick bath officials, U.S.P.H.S. officials, union officials, justice of peace, police and firemen, municipal workers, some teachers, the *colonia practicante* (nurse), most cafe and store owners, telephone operator.	Rural store and cafe owners, *mayordomos segundos*.
Veterans and public car drivers	
Quincalleros (ambulant venders), part-time artisans, lottery salesmen, clerks.	
Year-round employees of the sugar industry (e.g., foremen, railway workers)	
Cane workers	Cane workers and fishermen

For the cane workers, who are 70 percent of the male labor force, this total system has little relevance; their reference is not the *municipio* but the *barrio* in which only parts of the system obtain. The workers recognize a difference between themselves and those who live in the *pueblo,* calling themselves "*nosostros del barrio*" ("we of the *barrio*"). Even within this local unit there is no general intimacy, for rigid social distance is maintained between the workers and the managers.

> . . . no workers ever go to the homes of any of the hierarchy. Most completely separated is the head *mayordomo.* Social distance may be less great in the case of the lesser officials, yet the distinction between these men and the workers is great in terms of salary as well as in terms of education and general living standards, and while the managerial grouping may feel free to visit workers' homes on occasion, no such reciprocal feeling is enjoyed by the workers. The managerial grouping, moreover, seeks to perpetuate itself: a *mayordomo's* son will begin to learn his father's work while he is still in his teens, and he is usually expected to inherit the job if he wants it (Mintz:369).

The lack of informal interaction between these groups is due not only to status difference, but also to their representation of conflicting interests. The managers are concerned with milling cane efficiently and cheaply. The workers are interested in lengthening the employment period and raising their wages. Each group has a set of weapons to promote its position. For the workers, it is the slowdown, the union, and the strike. For the managers, it is the incentive system, the suspension of store credit during strikes, and the strikebreaker. Many workers cannot sustain the added poverty of a strike. Even ritual kinsmen, *compadres,* who are supposed to be bound by expectations of mutual support and obligation, may be on opposing sides durng a strike, one picketing, and the other strikebreaking.

Among *compadres,* who are almost always from the same class, there is some development of sharing and exchange labor, especially in housebuilding and in providing assistance at the birth of a child. But the economic system, based on wage labor on the estates, does not encourage the kinds of cooperative relationships characteristic of peasant areas. Kin ties, real and ritual, do not integrate the community. Recruitment to membership in the municipality is a matter of managerial decision.

Peasant and Plantation in Jamaica

Edith Clarke (1957) studied relationships between land tenure and domestic structures in three Jamaican villages: Sugartown, characterized by estate cultivation of cane; Mocca, a small village of subsistence horticulturalists; and Orange Grove, a town of relatively prosperous small farmers.

> The population of Sugartown is too large, too mixed and too mobile for the development of any strong community sense. What associations there are tend to be sectional and do not provide a relations system which involves continuous mutual cooperation and interdependence. The largest and most influential organization is the Trade Union, but it is an organization of sugar-labourers, and mainly confined to men. Other sectional associations are the Cane Farmers' Association and the Rice Growers' Association. The dances held occasionally on the Masquerade Ground bring another section of the community together—mainly the younger folk. The largest nonsectional gathering while we were there was on the occasion of the death of a prominent citizen. During the Nine Nights ceremonies which followed the funeral, a large and diverse section of the community participated at one time or another in the feasting and singing. But there is nothing in Sugartown to compare with the kinship solidarity of Mocca, or the opportunities which occur regularly in Orange Grove for the entire group, men, women and even children to meet together and act as a corporate whole (Clarke:24–25).

Sugartown differs from its Puerto Rican counterpart, Cañamelar, in the high percentage of persons who own the land on which their houses stand. These holdings have passed to the descendants of the original families, all of whom are related by ties of consanguinity or affinity. Kinship connections among the core of persons permanently resident in the village imply obligations of mutual assistance, looking after each other's children, and providing a home for kinsmen who return after a period away. The strangers who remain on the estate only during the cane harvest do not participate in these relationships of mutual dependence.

In economic activities, however, even the household is not corporate. A person's income is gained through individual wage labor on the plantation. Cooperation beyond the household is limited to housebuilding and is called partnership. In Orange Grove exchange-labor groups, known as morning sport, are used whenever the labor demands of agriculture exceed the capacities of the household. As in Morne-Paysan, the men of Orange Grove donated labor to the village, and combined to build a community hall, and the women prepared meals for the workers. In Mocca, plots are too small ever to need more labor than can be supplied by the household, but they too form groups, called matches, to aid in house construction.

Seasonal migrants do not come to Mocca and Orange Grove, nor do villagers leave in search of wage labor. Both villages are ethnically and economically homogeneous. Sugartown, on the other hand, is stratified economically, with estate managers at the top, shopkeepers in the middle, and laborers at the bottom. It is differentiated ethnically as well, and includes whites, East Indians, Chinese, and Negroes.

> Where Mocca and Orange Grove were integrated by kinship bonds and a common pattern of life, and organized to permit constant intercommunication, exchange of ideas and the transmission of approved modes of conduct, Sugartown presented itself as a collection of disparate un-assimilated and opposing aggregates. . . . [The features of diversity] were aggravated here by the high proportion of mobility in the population and the violence of the impact upon the relatively small group of permanent residents, of the immigrants and of the different behavior patterns and systems of values which they brought with them (Clarke:188).

Sugartown shares with Cañamelar the semiannual cycle of euphoric high wages during the harvest, allowing good eating, gambling, and visiting prostitutes, and dysphoric unemployment. In Mocca and Orange Grove cultivation continues throughout the year. Orange Grove, like Morne-Paysan, is geared to the Saturday market, and Saturday nights following a day of successful sales are times of general congregation and merriment.

Summary

This brief discussion is intended to give some idea of the kinds of agricultural villages found in the Caribbean. It is of course not exhaustive. The peasant villages of Morne-Paysan, Orange Grove, and Mocca share a number of characteristics. They show a high degree of communal activity, corporateness of household groupings, and a wide extension of extra-household kinship obligations. The populations of these villages are ethnically homogeneous and relatively stable. They do not regularly leave the village for outside employment, nor do outsiders enter in search of work. The sentiment often expressed, "we are all one family," tends to be literally true, for most of the villagers are descended from the original settlers, and joined to each other by marriage.

In Canalville peasant cultivation is valued above plantation labor, but the individual plots do not permit the luxury of complete escape from the estates. August Town, Canalville, and Tabara are characterized by more mobile populations, shifting from the farms to the sugar estates and, for August Town, to the bauxite fields. August Town and Tabara raise cash crops, rice, and tobacco respectively, rather than provisions. Canalville is the only one of these three in which exchange-labor groups are developed. Tabara is economically stratified, with specific activities associated with each stratum. Canalville is ethnically complex, with limited intermarriage which restricts a wide extension of kinship ties.

Sugartown and Cañamelar are devoted to sugar cane production on plantations. There are no peasants in these towns; the workers form agrarian proletariats without control over the processes of production and distribution, except as they are organized in labor unions. Class orientations are not only different but opposed: the elite tries to shorten the cane season, the workers try to lengthen it; the elite tries to keep costs down, the workers want wages increased. Opposition and conflict are expressed in strikes.

In Caribbean villages where landholdings are small and widely distributed, where labor is provided by the domestic group, and where the surplus crops are sold in local markets, the villagers are united by bonds of kinship, both actual and ritual, and mutual assistance. Where the land is held in great estates, and where the people must sell their labor in a factory situation, the village does not join the members in an interdependent matrix. The emphasis in peasant villages is on the household and occasional larger groupings for economic and ceremonial activities; in plantation villages the emphasis is on the individual and on the oppositions of the labor union and the managers' associations.

10

The Future of the Martiniquan Peasantry

AT BEST IT IS PROBLEMATIC that Morne-Paysan can maintain itself as a peasant village for many more years. While experts and officials speak of the desirability of diversifying agriculture, of the importance of supporting the peasant sector of the economy, and of making Martinique less dependent upon imported food, in fact it is large-scale agriculture which is expanding at the expense of the small producers. The most obvious factor is the decline in the total amount of land in peasant cultivation, and in the size of individual holdings. The cause of the latter is simple. We have seen that the patterns of inheritance involve fragmentation of holdings every generation. Families are large and all legitimate and recognized children inherit, and there are ways in which nonrecognized children share in the division as well. The problem of fragmentation is aggravated by the population explosion, which hit Martinique and the entire Caribbean as heavily as it did any other part of the world. More children are born alive; more survive infancy and childhood. And this increase is just beginning. Over the years the village was able to hold its own by exporting surplus population to the city and overseas. But the capacity of the city to sustain an increasing population is severely limited and has probably already been reached. Emigration to Cayenne, in South America, is a frequently debated panacea; from the French point of view, the benefits to Martinique in opening up the Guianian interior would not compensate for the tremendous initial expense of roads and matériel that would be required.

As the land becomes more and more crowded it becomes less and less productive. House plots encroach the fields. Declining productivity is a vicious cycle, for the low yield and consequent low market return do not permit the luxury of a long fallow period and soil rejuvenation. On tiny plots the peasant must farm intensively every year, losing nutrients and often the soil itself, as winds and rain wash off the earth. He cannot afford chemical fertilizer, and since there may be no fallow period, he is no longer able to trade pasturage for manure.

As land becomes less plentiful, it is also more expensive. We have seen that a farm of 3 hectares is a kind of rubicon; almost no one possessing less land is able to acquire that amount locally considered the minimum to support a household of two adults and four children with reasonable comfort. Land costs have sky-rocketed since the "discovery" of Morne-Paysan as a vacation area for people from the city, who seek relief from summer heat in the cooler highlands. At first the farmers looked on these vacationers with delight, for they promised a market within the village itself. But the effect was to have a number of landowners sell off pieces which they previously had rented out in *colonage.* More significant in the decline of peasant lands, however, is the removal of land from tenancy into pasturage. Several of the larger land owners are no longer renting out lands for cash or for a percentage of the harvest. Instead of distributing 20 hectares among as many *colons,* they have consolidated their holdings and put them in pasturage, selling milk and butchering meat. Two or three salaried laborers are all that is necessary to care for the herd, and the former *colons* have had to find new sources of employment. (The same thing happened in a different part of the island, when an estate gave up growing cane in favor of cattle and hundreds of people were thrown out of work.)

It would appear that as the amount of land in peasant production decreases, the returns from market sales for peasant produce increase. In part this has happened, and shoppers in the market complain about the rise in price of yams, taros, and other domestic foods. But the peasants have been faced in the last few years with competition from overseas. French vegetables, eggs, and frozen chickens are sold in Fort-de-France at the same and often lower prices than asked for local produce. Grocery shops now specialize in metropolitan vegetables and undersell the market. Some of the peasants have joined a marketing cooperative and are trying to reduce costs by combining their transportation and eliminating the *revendeuse* and her commission by selling directly to large consumers, like schools and hospitals. It is too early to judge whether they will be able to compete with the imported foods. It seems unlikely that they will to any great extent, and Martinique will become not more self-sufficient, but more dependent upon the metropole.

Peasants are in an economically precarious position because they are remote from political decision-making. They have neither the financial and parliamentary power of the planters, nor the syndical strength of the proletariat. From time to time one hears talk in Martinique of land reform. The left-wing parties have demanded that the government purchase large estates, and divide them into small lots for peasant production. Others have asked for settlement on public lands both in the central forest and on the *cinquante pas du roi,* the fifty paces of State-owned coastal zone that rings the island. Serious division of the estates is not likely as long as they continue to be profitable in sugarcane, bananas, pineapples, and pasturage, although an occasional plantation may pass into public hands. Settlement on public lands would be at best a temporary palliative, delaying the demise of peasantry perhaps as long as a generation.

Unless there are fundamental changes in the political status of Martinique, the process of proletarianization of the peasantry will continue. At times it may be slowed by providing the small planter with new crops, or credit, or fertilizer. But the long-range direction appears clear. Independence from the estates, so proudly claimed by maroons, who risked their lives to be free, and by freedmen, who refused to remain on the plantations after emancipation, will be remembered as just a past phase in the tormented history of the island.

Glossary

No attempt was made in these pages to render Creole phonetically wherever a French orthography appeared reasonable. For example, "sorcerer" is written *quimboiseur,* not *kâbwazur.* Some expressions are presented in a modified phonetic manner when they lack easy French rendition, as *ka u le,* (what do you want).

Béké: A white person born in Martinique; also called *blanc créole.* Descendants of the slave-owning planters, the *békés* are largely endogamous, and remain the economic aristocracy of the island. A white person born in France is a *métropolitain.*

Colon: In the seventeenth century, a planter; today, a sharecropper.

Colonage: Sharecropping.

Coup-de-main: Exchange labor group.

Débit de la régie: Licensed to sell spirits, that is, a bar.

Enfant légitime: A child born of married paents, or of parents who subsequently marry.

Enfant naturel: A child born of an unmarried mother.

Enfant reconnu: A child born of an unmarried mother, but recognized by its father, and given its father's name.

Engagé: Originally, a contract or indentured laborer; today, a bonded client of the devil, who receives nefarious powers in exchange for his soul.

Fête: Festival, holiday.

Franc: The official price of the *franc* during 1956–1958 varied from 350 to 490 to the U.S. dollar. In this book prices are given in old francs, as they are in Martinique today, although the franc has ben officially revalued 100 to 1.

Hectare: Unit of land measurement; 10,000 square meters, equal to 2.47 acres.

Ménage: Relationship of consensual cohabitation.

Métayage: Cash-tenancy of land. (Note: In France, *métayage* usually means share-cropping.)

Métropole: France.

Moitié-moitié: Division of harvest from land held in *colonage;* half to owner, and half to *colon.*

Quimbois: sorcery.

Revendeuse: Woman specialist in domestic marketing of peasant produce; also called *marchande* and *vendeuse.*

Veillée: Wake.

References

CÉSAIRE, AIMÉ, 1956, *Lettre à Maurice Thorez.* Paris: Présence Africaine.

*CLARKE, EDITH, 1957, *My Mother Who Fathered Me.* London: George Allen & Unwin Ltd.

FORDE, DARYLL, 1962, "Death and Succession: an Analysis of Yakö Mortuary Ritual." In *Essays on the Ritual of Social Relations,* Max Gluckman, ed. Manchester, England: Manchester University Press.

FOSBERG, FRANCIS R., ed., 1963, *Man's Place in the Island Ecosystem.* Honolulu: Bishop Museum Press.

FRAZIER, E. FRANKLIN, 1948, *The Negro Family in the United States,* revised edition. New York: Holt, Rinehart and Winston, Inc.

*HEARN, LAFCADIO, 1890, *Two Years in the French West Indies.* New York: Harper & Row, Publishers.

*HERSKOVITS, MELVILLE J. and FRANCES S., 1947, *Trinidad Village.* New York: Alfred A. Knopf, Inc.

HOROWITZ, MICHAEL M., 1963, "The Worship of South Indian Dieties in Martinique," *Ethnology,* Vol. 2, pp. 339–346.

———, and MORTON KLASS, 1961, "The Martiniquan East Indian Cult of Maldevidan," *Social and Economic Studies,* Vol. 10, pp. 93–100.

KEUR, JOHN Y. and DOROTHY L., 1960, *Windward Children.* Assen, Netherlands: Royal Vangorcum Ltd.

LOWENTHAL, DAVID, 1958, "The West Indies Chooses a Capital," *The Geographical Review,* Vol. 48, pp. 336–364.

MANNERS, ROBERT A., 1956, "Tabara: Subcultures of a Tobacco and Mixed Crops Municipality." In *The People of Puerto Rico,* by Julian H. Steward, and others. Urbana, Ill.: University of Illinois Press.

MÉTRAUX, ALFRED, 1951, *Making a Living in the Marbial Valley (Haiti).* Paris: UNESCO, Education Clearing House.

MINTZ, SIDNEY W., 1956, "Cañamelar: The Subculture of a Rural Sugar Plantation Proletariat." In *The People of Puerto Rico,* by Julian H. Steward, and others. Urbana, Ill.: University of Illinois Press.

———, 1960, "Peasant Markets," *Scientific American,* Vol. 203, No. 2, pp. 112–122.

———, 1964*a,* "Forward." In *Sugar and Society in the Caribbean,* by R. Guerra y Sánchez. Caribbean Series 7. New Haven, Conn.: Yale University Press.

———, 1964*b,* "Melville J. Herskovits and Caribbean Studies: a Retrospective Tribute," *Caribbean Studies,* Vol. 4, pp. 42–51.

* Recommended reading.

*Ortiz, Fernando, 1947, *Cuban Counterpoint.* New York: Alfred A. Knopf, Inc.

Perronnette, H., 1963, *Comment se nourir aux Antilles.* Fort-de-France, Martinique: Imprimerie Bezaudin.

Polanyi, Karl, Conrad M. Arensberg, and Harry W. Pearson, eds., 1957, *Trade and Market in the Early Empires.* New York: The Free Press of Glencoe, Inc.

Préfecture de la Martinique, 1964, *Monographie.* Fort-de-France, Martinique.

Revert, Eugéne, 1951, *La Magie antillaise.* Paris: Editions Bellenand.

Rouse, Irving, 1964, "Prehistory of the West Indies," *Science,* Vol. 144, pp. 499–513.

Simpson, George E., 1942, "Loup Garou and Loa Tales from Northern Haiti," *The Journal of American Folklore,* Vol. 55, pp. 219–227.

Skinner, Elliott P., 1955, *Ethnic Interaction in a British Guiana Rural Community: a Study in Secondary Acculturation and Group Dynamics.* Ph.D. Dissertation, Columbia University.

Smith, M. G., 1955, "A Framework for Caribbean Studies," *Caribbean Affairs.* Mona, Jamaica: University College of the West Indies, Extramural Department.

*———, 1962, *West Indian Family Structure.* Seattle: University of Washington Press.

*Smith, Raymond T., 1956, *The Negro Family in British Guiana: Family Structure and Social Status in the Villages.* London: Routledge & Kegan Paul Ltd.

*Steward, Julian H., and others, 1956, *The People of Puerto Rico.* Urbana: University of Illinois Press.

Vallee, F. G., 1955, "Burial and Mourning Customs in a Hebridean Community," *Journal of the Royal Anthropological Institute,* Vol. 85, pp. 119–130.

Wagley, Charles, 1957, "Plantation America: a Culture Sphere." In *Caribbean Studies: a Symposium,* Vera Rubin, ed., Mona, Jamaica: Institute of Social and Economic Research.

———, and Marvin Harris, 1955, "A Typology of Latin American Subcultures," *American Anthropologist,* Vol. 57, pp. 428–451.

Recommended Reading

The starred items on the list of references cited are recommended.

Very little has been written in English about the French West Indies—and that does not often commend itself to the serious reader. Lafcadio Hearn's *Two Years in the French West Indies,* 1890, is a happy exception. Written by a sympathetic journalist about a decade before Mt. Pelée erupted and destroyed much of what he described, the book is often reliable and always entertaining.

Much nonsense about Martinique has been written in French also. The following are good, and will well repay the effort in reading them. Leiris is a French anthropologist; the others are Martiniquans.

CÉSAIRE, AIMÉ, 1956, *Cahiers d'un retour an pays natal.* Paris: Présence Africaine.
A long and difficult poem about Césaire's return to Martinique after years in France. Césaire is a leader of the *négritude* movement which emerged in the French Caribbean and in the French-speaking countries in West Africa.

GLISSANT, ÉDOUARD, 1958, *La Lézarde.* Paris: Editions du Seuil.
A novel about young West Indian revolutionaries.

LEIRIS, MICHEL, 1955, *Contacts de civilisations en Martinique et en Guadeloupe.* Paris: UNESCO/Gallimard.
A perceptive appraisal of race relations in the French West Indies.

ZOBEL, JOSEPH, 1955, *La Rue Cases-Nègres.* Paris: Les Quatre Jeudis.
An intimate novel about rural life in Martinique.

The following works, all in English, deal with other parts of the Caribbean.

HERSKOVITS, MELVILLE J., 1937, *Life in a Haitian Valley.* New York: Alfred A. Knopf, Inc.
The first full ethnography in the insular Caribbean by an American anthropologist who was to dominate West Indian studies for twenty years.

KLASS, MORTON, 1961, *East Indians in Trinidad: a Study of Cultural Persistence.* (reprinted with changes 1988) Prospect Heights, IL: Waveland Press, Inc.
An award-winning analysis of a Trinidadian village, where formerly indentured laborers were able to reconstruct an Indian-based culture in a Creole society.

MINTZ, SIDNEY W., 1960, *Worker in the Cane: a Puerto Rican Life History.* New Haven, Conn.: Yale University Press.
A fascinating biography of a laborer on a sugar plantation.

SMITH, MICHAEL G., 1965, *The Plural Society in the British West Indies.* Berkeley, Calif.: University of California Press.
A collection of essays written over a ten-year period, including the important "A Framework for Caribbean Studies."

WILLIAMS, ERIC, 1944, *Capitalism and Slavery.* Chapel Hill, N.C.: The University of North Carolina Press.

An historical study of West Indian slavery by the man who became first (and current) Prime Minister of Trinidad and Tobago.

WOLF, ERIC, 1966, *Peasants.* Englewood Cliffs, N.J.: Prentice-Hall, Inc.

A superb analysis by an outstanding anthropologist who has worked among peasants in the Caribbean and Meso-America.